D0836468

UNDERSTANDING AND LOVING A PERSON WITH

SEXUAL
ADDICTION

UNDERSTANDING AND LOVING A PERSON WITH

SEXUAL ADDICTION

*Biblical and Practical Wisdom
to Build Empathy, Preserve Boundaries,
and Show Compassion*

STEPHEN ARTERBURN, M.Ed.
JASON B. MARTINKUS, M.A.
AND SHELLEY S. MARTINKUS

DAVID C COOK

transforming lives together

UNDERSTANDING AND LOVING A PERSON
WITH SEXUAL ADDICTION
Published by David C Cook
4050 Lee Vance Drive
Colorado Springs, CO 80918 U.S.A.

David C Cook U.K., Kingsway Communications
Eastbourne, East Sussex BN23 6NT, England

The graphic circle C logo is a registered trademark of David C Cook.

All rights reserved. Except for brief excerpts for review purposes,
no part of this book may be reproduced or used in any form
without written permission from the publisher.

The website addresses recommended throughout this book are offered as a
resource to you. These websites are not intended in any way to be or imply an
endorsement on the part of David C Cook, nor do we vouch for their content.

Details in some stories have been changed to protect
the identities of the persons involved.

Unless otherwise noted, all Scripture quotations are taken from the Holy Bible,
NEW INTERNATIONAL VERSION®, NIV®. Copyright © 1973, 2011 by Biblica, Inc.®
Used by permission. All rights reserved worldwide. NEW INTERNATIONAL VERSION®
and NIV® are registered trademarks of Biblica, Inc. Use of either trademark for the
offering of goods or services requires the prior written consent of Biblica, Inc.

LCCN 2017918220
ISBN 978-0-7814-1490-6
eISBN 978-0-8307-7221-6

© 2018 Stephen Arterburn
The Author is represented by and this book is published in association with the
literary agency of WordServe Literary Group, Ltd., www.wordserveliterary.com.

Cover Design: Amy Konyndyk

Printed in the United States of America
First Edition 2018

1 2 3 4 5 6 7 8 9 10

012918

Contents

Introduction

The term *sexual addiction* seems like such a cop-out when people who have been caught up in sexual sin use it. It can feel as though they are excusing all they have done by putting a label on it that absolves them of all responsibility. Questions such as these arise: "How can they blame their sin on an addiction?" "What does addiction have to do with sex anyway?" and "Isn't addiction what drug addicts have, not people who have sex?" It is easy to be confused by the term and the people who claim they have it.

In 1988, New Life Treatment Centers opened its first program in a psychiatric hospital, and we began to treat people who were destroying their lives with sex. The first patient was, to our surprise, a woman. She had been in an ongoing affair with a wealthy man who flew his own plane. They would take off, put it on autopilot, and have sex at five thousand feet. She knew it was wrong, but she could not stop—until she watched a program featuring a woman who shared all the same feelings she had experienced. Then she felt convicted, and that day she called the man and told him she would not be flying with him. As unbelievable as this will sound, the man ended up crashing the plane into the ocean off Long Beach, California, and died. If she had been in the plane, she would have died as well. When the woman saw the story on the news, she picked up the phone, called us, and decided it was time to get help. She knew she was a sex addict.

The big question many ask is, "Is it sin, or is it addiction?" My answer is always "Yes." It is "Yes" because I have never known an addict who was not involved in all sorts of sin, and I have never known a sinner who was not addicted to his or her sin of choice. They go hand in hand. But here is the headline: It does not matter whether a problem is a sin or an addiction. If it is a problem, it is the responsibility of the one with the problem to do something about it. And having an addiction is not a cop-out; it is something more than a mere problem or struggle.

When people have problems, they can get some counseling, mend their ways, and say they have dealt with them and move on. Addiction is different. If I am an addict, I can't just decide to stop and stay stopped. I need to get help. I need ongoing support. I need to attend meetings, work the steps, and stay in a lifelong program that ensures I will continue to grow and not fall back into my old ways.

Saying you are an addict means you are in greater need than just a person with a problem. The only time addiction is used as an excuse is in a courtroom when someone is trying to evade paying the consequences for unlawful behavior. What a slick attorney may try to do for a guilty client should not be confused with what a sex addict must do to get well.

If you have picked up this book, you have most likely been deeply hurt by the sexual behavior of another, just as I have been. And just like mine was, your fear might be that what happened once is just the beginning of many indiscretions. Your anger might be like mine was, so hot it feels as though it will burn through your stomach. Your sadness might be just like mine was, a belief that there is no hope for a great life in a great marriage. But there is no reason for despair. All things are possible, and the possibilities begin with this book.

I know of no one who has done a better job of helping more men than Jason Martinkus. He has struggled with his own sexual integrity and has gotten help, and now he helps thousands of men. He wrote this book with you in mind. He wants you to know what lies behind the addiction, and he and his wife and coauthor, Shelley, want you to know how to be helpful while taking care of your own needs and the needs of those close to you. All of us want this book to be a path to a new life with a recovering sex addict—or to beginning a new life separate from the addict if the addict refuses to get help. You have been on a painful journey, and we hope this extends it into healing territory that restores your faith, love, and hope.

—Stephen Arterburn

Preface

As I sit collecting my thoughts on how to write about sexual addiction, sexual integrity issues, the struggle to find freedom, and also the painful journey for the spouses of those affected, I wish I could provide a formula. I am compelled to craft a rubric within which every person fits and through which everyone can find comfort and hope for redemption. But as I work through that framework in my mind (picture a flowchart, if you will), I keep running into anomalous situations that break the model. The spectrum of struggle with sexual integrity issues is a wide one. For one group of people, the struggle is a one-night stand. They have no other systemic sexual integrity issues like pornography or masturbation. They do not have a lustful lifestyle. It almost seems like it's a fluke—and that's not to minimize the situation but to explain how far out of character it is. Then some men have long-standing, decades-old struggles with habitual sin in the form of porn and masturbation. They've never had or even contemplated a physical or emotional affair; perhaps it even scares them. But they've barely gone more than a month their whole lives without acting out. Some people go to massage parlors but not strip clubs, have emotional affairs but not physical ones, have sex with prostitutes but never someone they'll know for more than an hour. Some are trapped in fetishes, including violence and humiliation; some could never imagine such a thing.

The nuances to the patterns of acting out I've heard over the past thirteen years create so many scenarios that one size simply does not fit all. And when we add to that the broad range of responses and experiences for those who love the struggler, the framework for recovery and restoration gets even more complicated. Some wives love their husbands with extravagant grace and mercy when they find out about their struggles. Some of those same gracious wives are just in denial and not willing to acknowledge the pain and devastation they've experienced. Some wives immediately divorce, while others are willing to give it time, to wait and see. Some children have a newfound respect for a parent when the truth comes out. For others, it creates a divide that seems impossible to bridge. For extended family or in-laws, when the truth is known, it can create the most awkward dynamic at Christmas. They struggle with forgiveness and figuring out how to act at the dinner table. Do they throw the whole bowl of mashed potatoes at the person or just smack them with one dollop? For some, the family dynamics actually ease because there is no longer an elephant in the room that nobody wants to talk about. The reactions and subsequent dynamics of family run the gamut.

There are also a multitude of scenarios within a marriage. Perhaps a spouse disclosed his struggle before engagement, and the couple has had that conversation a thousand times over decades. It's old. Others have never had that conversation, and the wife finds out for the first time through a call from her ob-gyn delivering news of an STI. I've seen wives who got that call on their honeymoon and wives who got that call in their fifties.

Background is yet another X factor. People have a common conception that a person struggling with sexual addiction must have been sexually abused. But in my experience, it's equally as realistic that they were not. Some grew up with a chaotic, abusive, and neglectful childhood, others with Ward and June Cleaver.

You see my point? All these factors together create a diversity of situations that we simply cannot put into clear-cut categories.

When I was in the corporate world, white papers were popular. A *white paper* was a collection of best practices for a given subject. Experts in a field would, based on their vast experience, create a document that spelled out the most effective and efficient ways to handle situations to create the best possible outcome. While the document didn't list every nuance and how to adapt the practices in every unique situation, it gave a framework that could then be customized and adopted within an organization. My hope for this book is similar.

As badly as I want to draw nice straight lines to categorize the struggle and recovery, the page is full of squiggly lines. There is no formula. There are, however, some commonalities. There are themes both in the patterns of acting out and in the patterns of response for those who care about the person struggling. And there are some guidelines and principles that, while they need to be adapted to each unique situation, can provide a framework to help you reach the best possible outcome.

CHAPTER ONE

Shared Experiences

If you find yourself living in the aftermath of the disclosure or discovery of sexual betrayal, I am so sorry. The pain, confusion, and hopelessness are real and overwhelming. The roller coaster of emotions can feel almost unbearable—one day you may feel seemingly normal and the next like it's nearly impossible to get out of bed. There are moments in the day when you feel grounded and calm, followed by hours poring over memories, conversations, and situations, trying to figure out how this all happened. This is normal. You are not alone. Let me share a couple of stories with you of people who've been through similar struggles. I want you to know that there is hope and that redemption is possible.

John and Jenny

John and Jenny were in their early forties and had been married for twenty years. They had two kids in elementary school. Life seemed to be what it should. They were involved in their church, navigating careers, and trying to do the best they could. As the story often goes, John had grown increasingly close to a coworker. In the close quarters of the work environment, once seemingly innocuous conversations became insidious. The subject matter moved from professional to personal and then to intimate. Oddly, yet not uncommonly, they connected primarily over their faith journeys. After all, they were both in ministry at a church. Along the path of life, John's faith journey had taken twists and turns, the way all such journeys do, and he had become disenchanted with God. It was the same story for the coworker. She got it. She could relate. They had talked about it often and at length. In stark contrast, his wife, Jenny, really didn't want to hear it anymore. It's not that she didn't have compassion for John or that she didn't want him to find peace with it. She just wanted to enjoy the moment and not worry about deep things.

Eventually, there was a hug. Then there was a kiss. The secrecy intensified to cover the frequency of conversations, texts, and meetings. And finally, there was sexual intimacy. John was instantly paralyzed with fear, guilt, and shame. He ended the affair on the spot. He didn't want to leave Jenny or his kids. He didn't really want to be in this adulterous relationship in the first place, but it had inundated him when he was at work every day and intoxicated him once he was in her presence. I'm not excusing it; I'm simply explaining it. He concluded that he would find a new job, work hard to make things better at home, and take the secret to his grave. If things improved and he and Jenny got on the same page, there would be no further damage done. Or so he thought.

After a couple years, things weren't better, and John and Jenny landed in my office. John had told Jenny the truth, and they were dealing with the fallout. Unlike most spouses hit by a grenade like this, Jenny wasn't devastated. She wasn't raging angry. She was mostly calm, barely tearful. She dismissed it with "these things happen." Sometimes she would make accusations about him—about the way he tried to love her or handle their relationship. He didn't want to seem defensive and hurt her, so he wouldn't say anything about it. Eventually, he called me outside of sessions to say, in a heartfelt and tender way, that what she was saying made no sense. He couldn't even imagine where she was stretching to come up with some of the stories; even the language was foreign to him. She described their conversations with words he didn't even have in his vocabulary! In a twilight-zone kind of way, he felt guilty and ashamed of his actions, yet he was also confused because it seemed as though, at times, she described a life and reality other than their own.

Through our sessions working on grieving, restoring trust, and creating a deeper intimacy in light of the affair, we kept hitting a wall. Jenny wouldn't let her guard down. She just wouldn't let herself receive his love. It was like she wanted desperately to be intimate and deeply connected but kept hanging on to an immature idea of adulthood and a fairy-tale concept of love and relationships. Then the truth came out.

Jenny was sexually addicted. She had, for the better part of the last decade, been sexting, chatting with and exchanging pictures with men, and watching pornography. She had purchased attire to wear for other men and had an emotional affair with a member of the family. She broke down in tears and shame as she told the story. No wonder she wouldn't engage John's faith journey; she was off the rails of her own. She couldn't receive his love because she was living within her own shame and guilt. She felt like a monster. In fact, some of what she described as their reality was actually that of her online relationships. Her worlds were colliding at times without her even realizing it. For John, the dots finally connected.

Now, I don't want to gloss over the difficulty of the restoration process, but Jenny and John ultimately landed in a healing and intimate place. Today, they enjoy each other's company, are navigating parenting and faith together, and, having been through the trenches, retain a confidence in what their relationship can withstand.

Sometimes the story doesn't have a shocking reveal. I've walked with numerous couples who had no deep dark secrets. They didn't land at some point in life where a bomb went off and they had to cull through the shrapnel and destruction of their relationship. Instead, they experienced death by a thousand cuts.

In one of those situations, the husband's disclosures began during dating. Right from the get-go, he wanted to be honest, so he told her about his pornography addiction. He admitted the severity, was open about getting help, and was genuinely well-intentioned about it all. Feeling thankful for his openness and transparency, she concluded that he would willingly talk about it if necessary, so she didn't need to ask about it. Through their engagement, he would periodically confess, through generic code, that he had violated their relationship with porn. "I struggled" was one phrase. "I looked at pictures" was another one. "I had a hard day with temptation and lust" was more spiritual sounding. Each time, she found comfort in his honesty and obvious commitment to keep fighting.

They married, and over the first four or five years, he continued the pattern. A couple times a year, he would confess. At this point, it had become casual. He would throw it in with dinner table talk: "I went to the office, worked on spreadsheets, had meetings, then left the office and stopped at the grocery store for milk, and also looked at pictures today." The nonchalant way he would weave it into conversations again gave his wife some security. She didn't like that he still struggled with it, but she figured it must be fairly under control since he wasn't making a big deal about it.

Over the next decade, it was the same story, different day. Only something changed for her: she decided to start asking questions. She began asking what he was actually looking at, in detail, and how often. She asked if he was masturbating as well. And she asked who or what he was thinking about when he did. And how often. It turned out that his struggle was weekly, and it was with same-sex pornography and bondage pornography. Further, he was fantasizing about people she knew—both men and women. She tried again to roll with it. He described it with a tone of normalcy, and she accepted it. She was committed to praying for him and considered it his journey, not something for her to involve herself in much.

Fast-forward twenty years. When he would casually confess, she began feeling more violated. She started to read up on the subject and concluded that it was a much bigger deal than he had let on—even more than he wanted to believe for himself. She began to see the patterns of how it affected their intimacy and relationship. She saw connections to his depression and changes in mood. She started asking more frequently how he was doing. She would use code too: "How's the struggle today?" or "Did you have a *good* day?" He would answer honestly every time, but it was almost always an answer of defeat.

She loved him deeply and wanted the best for him, so she finally insisted he get help. He balked for years. She distanced herself, protecting her heart. She stopped asking; he stopped confessing. They both knew it was more than just a "struggle," and the end result was the erosion of their relationship. By the time the kids were out of the house, they were roommates at best.

When they came to see me, they were individually hopeless. He couldn't picture a life without acting out again. Her presence was perfunctory; she was just there because I asked her to be, not because she had any inclination their marriage could be restored. Death by a thousand cuts.

But their story doesn't end there. After attending an Every Man's Battle workshop and connecting with a group in his local church, he finally decided enough was enough. Perhaps more accurately, he finally caught a glimpse of hope that his acting out wasn't inevitable. A year into counseling, he was living with integrity. Her trust was beginning to return, and she actually began to find her voice again. When they stopped coming to my office, they weren't fixed, and the process wasn't final, but they were looking toward a future date to renew their vows.

Jason and Shelley

Since we're talking stories, I also want you to know ours. Again, while it may not be a one-for-one fit, I hope you'll find connection points to your experience.

Shelley grew up in a Christian home with fairly strict ground rules about sex and sexuality. She survived her teenage years with no promiscuity or even experimentation. She prayed for her future husband (me) to have done the same. Shelley did it "right." When we met, I was really interested in her. Enjoying my pursuit and attention, she lowered her bar. I had a past: a few sexual experiences and a "struggle" with pornography that was mostly over with—at least, that is how I told the story. She made the exception, and we fell in love.

We graduated from college, got married in a big Texas wedding, and started to ride off into the sunset together. That lasted about three months until I was unfaithful to her. I was back into porn and chat rooms, and I had an affair. She had no clue. It happened sixteen more times over the next several years. Between emotional and physical affairs, I would binge on pornography and masturbate. When I wasn't acting out and I had a streak going, I was actually fun to be around and loving toward her. We had really good moments and enjoyed parts of our life together. But when I was sucked into the shame vortex after having acted out in some way, I was a jerk. I was lazy and uninvolved. I withheld love from Shelley and treated her with disdain—unless she was having sex with me. I pressured her a lot for that. Sometimes I would even use biblical language to guilt her into the act.

She thought she was crazy.

How in the world could the guy she fell in love with be this way after "I do"? It was a tale of two worlds, and she never knew which version of Jason she was going to get. Shelley was too embarrassed to say anything to friends or family. It would prove she wasn't perfect—which was a core vow she had made to herself: to always be perfect. Instead of getting help, she just pondered in the confines of her own mind whether this was how life and marriage were supposed to be. Perhaps it was all a big lie, and everyone who was married had the same experience. On stage, in public, life was good and exciting and the way it should be. But behind the curtain were bitterness, resentment, disappointment, and increasing discontent. Shelley knew something was wrong. In moments of clarity, she would center herself and hold on to the fact that she knew things weren't right. She would ask me if everything was okay and usually get a "Yeah, things are fine. Why?" response. On occasion, I would blame and criticize her. Lacking any true self-awareness, I would take her question as an opportunity to assuage my guilt and shame by shifting the responsibility for my marital dissatisfaction onto her—never mind that I hadn't kept up my end of the agreement.

Shelley could never quite make sense of the things happening to me either. She's not a techie person, so when my computers had frequent viruses, she just naively took my word that I had to reinstall the operating system over and over. I lost my job because of my acting out, but my cover story was plausible enough. She was confused but, like any well-intentioned wife who wants desperately to trust her husband, convinced herself to ignore the contradictions in my explanation.

I often tell the story of throwing a company-owned laptop in a dumpster, thinking it would cure my addiction, then lying to Shelley (and my employer) about how it had "gotten stolen." She kept going through the scenario, asking questions about how it all happened, as if she were on *CSI* or something. I just kept stringing out the story with more nonsense. She genuinely wanted to understand, but I kept confounding the story. She finally had to let it go because she couldn't keep feeling crazy.

Our whole situation began to reach a boiling point when my behavior got more unpredictable, more suspicious, erratic, and unexplainable. Shelley suspected an affair. When she approached the subject, I denied it. I minimized her concerns, shut down her inquiries, and slammed the door on any ongoing conversations about it. Eventually, I admitted there was almost an affair (a total lie), but I blamed it all on her. I feel an ache in my bones even writing this now. I hate how I treated her.

For the better part of the following year, I retreated further into myself and she moved further away from herself. She lost herself. She changed her hair, her makeup, her wardrobe. She booked trips for us to places she thought would make me happy and make me love her. She tried to be more sexual, taking more initiative and ultimately feeling more like an object than my wife. It still didn't fix things. Shelley finally called my affair partner and found out the truth. She confronted me about it. I lied all the way through it and tried to make her feel like she was making it all up. But she wasn't. And she knew it this time.

When the truth finally did come out, it was incredibly validating for her. It was painful, horrible, and devastating, but it also connected so many dots. It proved she really wasn't crazy—naive, but not crazy. The explanation—sexual addiction—was not comforting. In fact, she felt it was dismissive. You can't just chalk up all this devious, sinful behavior to an illness. And she was right—you can't. There is way more to it than that.

With that, our healing began, both individually and collectively. We entered into a sanctification process at that point. God wanted to change me from the inside out. We began counseling and focused on my character issues, accountability, and reengaging faith. It was hard. *So* hard. Here in Colorado, they do these big ice sculptures during the winter. They'll take a huge square block of ice and create a masterfully carved and detailed piece of art. The tools they use to finish the sculpture are small, narrow, fine-edged chisels. *But they start with chainsaws.* That's kind of how our process began. I was a big block of ice (a fitting metaphor), and God was taking off huge chunks with His chainsaw; pieces of ice were flying everywhere! Shelley kept her distance, watching and waiting to see the final form. She made the decision to stay in the marriage. She rode out the transition from chainsaws to chisels.

We began telling our story, ministering to other people. I felt called out of corporate and into ministry. Fast-forward through ups and downs, setbacks and leaps forward, and thirteen years later, here we are. Shelley helps wives around the globe; I have the privilege of helping men and marriages, teaching workshops, and being a part of this book.

Granted, I skipped a lot of stuff to get to the end of the story! Both pain and beauty are built into that process. We'll talk more about that as we go through the chapters that follow. What I want to do is give you a little picture of hope and redemption. We're not special. We're no more qualified or capable or usable than anyone else. God does miraculous work, over the long run, in the lives of willing people. That's what He's done with us. That's what He can do with you. Regardless of the severity of addiction or struggle, regardless of how far gone it feels like things are, there is hope. Things can be different. Our hope is that this book will serve as a white paper. While geared toward wives who are trying to navigate the journey with a struggling husband, nearly all the principles can be applied inversely. Also, at the end of the book, we've included a chapter to help you know what steps to take if the person struggling is a child or young adult in your house. We want to give you guidelines that are adaptable to your situation so you can experience the best God has for you and the people you love who are struggling.

CHAPTER TWO

Is Sexual Addiction Real?

Sexual addiction is a controversial topic. For Shelley, it was a label representing an excuse—a justification—for hurtful and sinful behavior. For me, it was a huge relief! If there was a name for this malady, then I couldn't be the only one who has struggled like this. Further, it meant there might be an answer, a solution. It represented hope for me. For many men, it is just such a beacon of hope.

For some, it is a scarlet letter, and admitting they are struggling is incredibly difficult. In a recent survey, the Barna Group concluded that one in three Americans searches for pornography at least once per month.[1] But that statistic may not even be accurate, given that what constitutes pornography is highly subjective. Barna asked the survey respondents to define pornography, and they had five different answers with nearly the same percentage. The answers ranged from content to intent.[2] Further, some people debate about whether pornography use is a problem. It all amounts to a very ambiguous and opaque landscape. The idea of sexual addiction is certainly debatable. Let's take a look at some common ways it shows up in society.

Sexual Addiction in the News

In the past decade, sex addiction has gotten a fair amount of publicity thanks to celebrities. Before you even read the names I'll list, several probably come to mind. Tiger Woods, Michael Douglas, Anthony Weiner, David Duchovny, Charlie Sheen, Jesse James, and Harvey Weinstein are but a few. These folks drew attention to the subject, even if they didn't don the official label of *addict*. Treatment programs for sexual addiction gained national notoriety once the media found out where these stars were getting help. Raising awareness of the issue is certainly positive, and some say any publicity is good publicity, but I disagree on this one. The coverage has multiple unintended consequences.

Unfortunately, for most of these folks, the media portrayed their struggles in a scandalous way. Media coverage painted the issue in a light that discredited the severity of it and in some cases even romanticized their activities as just some playboys getting caught. Rather than acknowledging the pain, devastation, and internal chaos for someone struggling, it became tabloid fodder. The covers of trash magazines used it as the latest nonsense to shock shoppers in grocery store checkout lines. I personally have felt appalled and insulted by what I've seen and read. The internal sense of duplicity, powerlessness, and hopelessness can be overwhelming—for me and others like me—to the point of causing suicidal thoughts. I imagine that was the case for some of those folks too, but that side of things didn't get much attention.

Another myth of the media portrayal is that it's all about sex—physical sex. Some of the celebrities dealt with pornography, but sexual escapades far overshadowed that in media coverage. However, there is much more involved in sex addiction. Sex and porn are aspects, but there are emotional affairs, fetishes, and nuances to the types of porn, to the people involved, and to the way and time when someone acts out.

All that leads to another issue: this struggle is about sex. The media, and perhaps even some of the people featured, portrays the whole thing as if these folks are systemically just fine. They just happen to have this one area of life that's out of order. But otherwise, everything is fine.

Bull.

You don't grossly misuse your sexuality when there aren't systemic character issues. The underlying character issues that drive sexual acting out are woven into the very fabric of our existence. You can't parse them. The tentacles of those issues touch every area of our lives—work, home, parenting, marriage, relationships, friendships, hobbies, faith, and so on. Consequently, another myth the media perpetuates is the quick fix. The mocha hits the fan; it hits the news; they duck out of their lives to go to treatment; then, sometime later, they reenter the lives they left, all fixed. We hear next to nothing about their ongoing recovery work. It's not that they owe us the behind-the-scenes look at their lives, but they often make a public statement on the front end. Beyond that quick-fix feel, it also sends the message that life as you know it doesn't have to change. Tiger's still got his first mistress: golf. Douglas kept doing movies. James still went on with TV and mechanics. Anthony Weiner returned from his first round of help to run for mayor of New York City. We all have seen the fallout in these folks' marriages, which I'll address shortly. But the overarching themes of their lives don't seem to change much. The lives of the people I know who've found radical redemption look vastly different in so many ways, not just professionally.

Last but not least is the unfortunate fallout for the people associated with the person struggling. The public gets little of the real impact on wives, mothers, fathers, and kids. Likewise, the flip side of the coin is true—we get next to no glimpse of hope and redemption. I see so many stories of reconciliation, but the high-profile people the media covers usually end in tragic split-ups. The media coverage has done a grave injustice, I believe, in not giving a realistic idea of what the process can look like.

Okay, I'm off the soapbox.

Sexual Addiction in the Counselor's Office

The term *sexual addiction*, as it relates to a diagnosis, is debated among the therapeutic community as well. Some counselors refute that sexual addiction is real. Alternatively, therapists who want to help with sexual addiction can take advantage of the current groundswell of teaching, training, and certifications in this area. Ironically, however, the governing medical body that identifies, researches, certifies, and names disorders does not consider it a bona fide disorder! If you've begun reaching out to the therapeutic community for help, you have probably been introduced to the debate. For the sake of our conversation and this book, I want to explain how these entities determine their opinions and how to move forward with this information.

Diagnostic and Statistical Manual of Mental Disorders

The *Diagnostic and Statistical Manual of Mental Disorders* (*DSM*) is the bible of mental unhealthiness. It is the authoritative text that classifies and defines mental disorders, and virtually every clinician in the United States uses it. Any therapist with a counseling degree is familiar with it. The *DSM* is compiled by the American Psychiatric Association (APA), a large organization comprised of mostly M.D. and Ph.D. individuals involved in clinical care, research, and academics. If you check out their website, you'll see the posted goal of this consortium of experts is "to ensure humane care and effective treatment for all persons with mental illness, including substance use disorders."[3]

In practice, the *DSM* outlines the criteria, symptoms, and conditions that must be met for a mental health diagnosis to be made. The APA has done a masterful job through countless hours of research and expert input of defining what is and is not a valid criterion for a disorder. As a society and culture today, we have a tendency to use some of this psychotherapeutic language casually. People will accuse someone who is selfish of being a narcissist, or someone who is fickle or moody will be labeled bipolar. Even the term *addiction* has become watered down and used to describe our relationships to any number of things from tacos to TV shows. Most often, though, people use this language pejoratively rather than descriptively. The *DSM* ensures that these types of labels are appropriately applied by individuals who've been trained to apply them and only under the operating principle that it is in the highest and best interest of the patient or client. Functionally, for what it's worth, these diagnoses are also what insurance companies use when calculating reimbursement rates for service providers.

DSM and Sexual Addiction

The *DSM* does *not* recognize sexual addiction as a bona fide disorder and thus does not offer a subsequent diagnosis. The *DSM* is revised periodically, and any new information and research are taken into account. Updates are made with the advent of new findings; new diagnoses are added, and existing ones are refined. The most recent revision of the *DSM* was published in 2013. Ostensibly, the research contributing to 2013 revisions began in 2000. Over the course of thirteen years, the research on sexual addiction was apparently inconclusive. It is fair to say that the experts could not find enough evidence to conclude a diagnosis was warranted.

That said, the *DSM* has for the entirety of its existence identified some sort of sexual dysfunction. The folks who assimilate all the research and information have long noted that there are sexual behaviors that fall outside the norm. The problem arises when these researchers try to decide what norm or whose norm to follow. This makes developing the criteria and subsequent diagnosis difficult. Societal, religious, scientific, and cultural norms may, in any given aspect of sexuality, all align or all disagree. What is considered sexually dysfunctional in one culture may be entirely appropriate in another. What one religion says is sexually out of bounds may be part and parcel of another's worship practices. Beyond that, scientific norms based on physiology and biology are a factor.

After all this consideration, you can see how challenging it can be to determine criteria for a disorder or diagnosis. As such, the *DSM* does have a category titled "hypersexual disorder." Under this heading, behaviors we would typically consider associated with sexual addiction are listed, including problematic use of masturbation, pornography, cybersex, and so on.

Clinical Debate

There is certainly debate among clinicians as to whether sex addiction is real.

In fact, at the time of this writing, we are on the heels of a controversial statement issued by a group of therapists regarding sex addiction. On November 29, 2016, the American Association of Sexuality Educators, Counselors, and Therapists (AASECT), an organization that issues a certification titled "sex therapist," issued this position statement:

> AASECT recognizes that people may experience significant physical, psychological, spiritual and sexual health consequences related to their sexual urges, thoughts or behaviors. AASECT recommends that its members utilize models that do not unduly pathologize consensual sexual behaviors. AASECT 1) does not find sufficient empirical evidence to support the classification of sex addiction or porn addiction as a mental health disorder, and 2) does not find the sexual addiction training and treatment methods and educational pedagogies to be adequately informed by accurate human sexuality knowledge. Therefore, it is the position of AASECT that linking problems related to sexual urges, thoughts or behaviors to a porn/sexual addiction process cannot be advanced by AASECT as a standard of practice for sexuality education delivery, counseling or therapy.[4]

That's sort of hard for me to follow. My first thought was, "What the heck are *pedagogies*?" So in simple terms, here's what I understand them to be saying:

> Sex addiction isn't real. If you believe in sex addiction, you may not
> know enough about sexuality and thus might incorrectly assume
> something considered sexually "normal" to be "abnormal" as part
> of an addiction.

That's fair, I suppose, especially if you have a very humanistic view of sexuality. But if you have a biblical view of sexuality, I would submit this view would quickly detour from what is right, true, and good by God's design. But that's a later chapter. And by the way, *pedagogies* are theories and practices of education/teaching.

In the month after the AASECT issued the statement, other organizations, both faith-based and secular, have issued their own statements debating, debunking, and disagreeing with AASECT's stance (the International Institute for Trauma and Addiction Professionals, as well as the Association of Partners of Sex Addicts Trauma Specialists). Consequently, the issue itself has gotten quite a bit more attention on the treatment side, not just the symptom side, which is a positive thing.

A Different Perspective

So what do we do with all this information? If you're reading this book, you know and probably love someone who is struggling sexually, and regardless of what it's called, his struggles are causing pain and heartache! What the medical world concludes is or isn't real and what people actually experience can be two different things. The stance a counseling organization takes on something can be vastly different than the stance we take based on our lived experiences.

In my opinion, what we personally deem problematic in our lives, relative to our own norms and values and within our faith frameworks, is far more important. As we personalize our stories and the challenge of being in a relationship with someone struggling with sexual integrity issues, the medical and clinical definitions become moot at some point: our lived experiences provide sufficient definition. With that in mind, I absolutely believe sex addiction is real. How it manifests in someone's life might not meet the medical world's criteria. However, let me give you a different perspective.

While in school at Denver Seminary, I heard a professor say there are three key characteristics of addiction. They've stuck with me because they described my life to a *T*. He said something might be an addiction if it is

1. compulsive—the person can't seem to stop, even with the best intentions;
2. mood altering—the person uses the activity to change the way he feels, especially to numb or escape painful emotions; and
3. life disrupting—it negatively impacts the person physically, spiritually, relationally, financially, professionally, or in other areas of life.

When you think about it, what could we use addictively in our lives? Just about anything! Food, exercise, work, the Internet, Facebook, and so on. Is it that much of a stretch to say we might use sex addictively too?

A Better Definition

Semantically, we have a limited definition when we use the word *sex*. What do we mean by sex? We tend to think of the physical act. But if we expand the word to *sexual*, we broaden what might be included in the definition. When we speak of things that are sexual, it encompasses all aspects of our sexual nature: the acts, the physical touch that leads to the acts, the emotions that lead to the touch, and even the electric feelings we get that spark it all. It includes a holistic view of what sexual intimacy entails. This means we have to consider our minds, hearts, bodies, and souls.

Rather than identify this struggle as *sex addiction*, I prefer to use the term *sexual addiction*. I believe this is more fitting. Sexual addiction means using some aspect(s) of our sexual nature in a compulsive, mood-altering, life-disrupting way. In addition, I prefer to use the language *struggling with sexual addiction* or *struggling with sexual integrity issues* rather than *sex addict* or *sexual addict*. The reason has to do with identity. Labels and categories like *addict* can become one's identity. Yet, as followers of Jesus, our identities are rooted in who He is, not what we've done. I believe we can be free from our addictions (Gal. 5:1). That does not mean we will never experience temptation to don the old yoke of addiction. I expect temptation to be around till death. What it *does* mean is that our identities are in Christ, not our addictions. I've never appreciated the model of recovery that requires people to identify themselves as addicts when they introduce themselves. I get why they do it—it is imperative to stay grounded in the reality of our struggles and not live in overconfidence or denial. But as believers in Jesus, our identities are more than the sum total of our bad behaviors. Our identity is in our position as dearly loved, infinitely valuable sons and daughters of the living God.

Sexual Addiction Is Not about Sex

It is important for us to understand what sexual addiction is really about. When we broaden the definition from *sex* to *sexual* addiction, we give ourselves the opportunity to break from the current paradigm. As it stands, between the nomenclature and the myths created by media and culture, there are a couple of insinuations that miss the heart of the struggle.

High Sex Drive

We can begin with the myth that someone struggling with sex addiction has a higher-than-normal sex drive. This has its roots in *nymphomania*—the idea that someone needs sex very frequently. While the frequency desired might fall outside what is considered normative, it is an issue connected to biology. However, the core of it has more to do with a person's whole being (mind, heart, body, and soul) than it does with his inherent natural biological order. Let's look at one facet of the biological aspect.

Neural Chemistry

Neural chemistry is the primary area where this addiction is biological in nature. When we engage sexually, a host of chemicals are released in the brain: dopamine, epinephrine, adrenaline, serotonin, oxytocin, vasopressin, and endogenous opiates just to name a few. The neurochemical dopamine, along with endogenous opiates, plays an integral role in sexual addiction. Dopamine is responsible for two key functions. First, it drives novelty. It puts our brains on high alert for experiences that are new and exciting. Second, it drives satiation. Dopamine propels us toward feeling satisfied.

That feeling of satisfaction is a direct result of opiate activation in the brain. It can be described as a sort of euphoria. It's the sense of release, relief, and calm that sets in upon ejaculation. In the brain of someone sexually addicted, both dopamine and opiate activation are out of calibration. The release and reception of the chemicals are out of balance. The by-product is that the brain develops a tolerance to the stimulation, thus developing stronger and more intense sexual cravings.[5] As Steve and company write in *Every Young Man's Battle*, we end up with a sumo-sized sex drive.[6]

While someone sexually addicted may desire sex frequently, it is more a function of distorted neural chemistry than natural drive. Further, that distortion leads to the escalation of his addiction. In other words, the acting out gets worse. What characterizes "worse" is unique to each individual. For some, it means the frequency of porn-viewing episodes will increase. Or instead of a regular rhythm of half-hour episodes, it becomes less frequent binges lasting hours each time. Unfortunately, as it pertains to pornography, many people report searching for and viewing things they never imagined getting caught up in. The depth of depravity is endless, and the bounds of available content are scary.

For others, the behavior becomes increasingly risky. On one hand, the risk is to their livelihood. They do things that could potentially get them fired from their jobs if they are caught or even guarantee they can never work in the same field again. Their behavior ups the ante to the point where being found out would require moving to an entirely different state. The escalation sometimes moves offline, from pornography to prostitutes or affairs, putting health and physical well-being in jeopardy. This is especially scary for someone married to a sexual addict. Too many wives I talk to are recipients of a sexually transmitted infection. The reality is that some wives are at risk of HIV just due to the bad decisions of their husbands.

Another unfortunate faulty belief is that a person with this affliction walks around like a sex-crazed monster or pervert, always on the prowl for a consenting, or perhaps even nonconsenting, victim. The unintended consequence of this is vilification of the person struggling. That person then internalizes the message of being a monster, and as we'll discuss shortly, the message becomes a part of the trap keeping the addicted person ensnared.

Getting Physical

Finally, an insinuation that limits our understanding is that sex addiction is merely about the physical act. It unfortunately disregards all the emotional impacts of engaging one's sexuality. For example, feelings like acceptance, peace, belonging, love, value, worth, affirmation, power, and adequacy are woven into the experience of sexual intimacy. Any or all of these can be intoxicating, alluring, and potentially addictive in themselves. Many of the folks I've had the privilege of walking with, and even I myself as part of my own addictive journey, have acted out in the form of an emotional experience. As a heroin addict longs for another hit and injects the needle into his arm, so does a sexual addict crave the medicinal and intoxicating feelings associated with sex.

What I'm getting at here is that in order to extend grace and love to someone struggling with a sexual addiction, we must dismantle what we see and understand at face value. I am convinced that as you delve deeper into the heart and mind of someone struggling, you'll begin to see him in a different, more compassionate and empathic light.

Shelley's Thoughts

Before the full truth came out, I convinced myself that our sex life was to blame for the strife we experienced in our marriage. It didn't help matters that I believed making sure Jason was fully satisfied sexually was one of my top duties as a Christian wife. It also didn't help, as Jason mentioned in the last chapter, that when he was feeling guilt and shame over his acting out, he would assuage this shame by telling me I needed to be sexier.

Thus when Jason finally gave me back some of my dignity by sharing the full truth with me, it was very, very difficult to convince me that his issues weren't about sex. Besides, it's called a sexual addiction. Little did I know the issue had to do with intimacy, or being fully known.

It took many months, possibly even years, for me to fully understand that Jason's choices were much less about sex and much more about looking for a way to be fully known without the full risk of rejection. Think about it—the pornography

Jason was viewing would never reject him. Only when he was ready to be done would he shut the computer screen. Same with the women he met up with—he was in charge and told them what he wanted, not the other way around. He made sure of that from the get-go. In this way, Jason felt a small bit of love, acceptance, and connection—but it was fleeting and fraudulent, which left him emptier than before and searching for more.

Please know that just as it was for me, it could take months or even years to fully believe at a heart level that your spouse's choices weren't about sex but rather about his search for true intimacy.

CHAPTER THREE

Underpinnings of Sexual Addiction

The internal world of someone struggling with sexual integrity issues is usually a volatile, tumultuous place. A war rages inside him, with good and evil squaring off against each other. Good will win out, but the effects are momentary. Someone might go a few days or a week without acting out sexually. But fear and anxiety quickly replace the temporary relief and celebration, because it seems as though the next slip is inevitable. That fear gives way to hopelessness and depression. Another round of acting out will follow—thus guilt, shame, and conviction set in again.

We fight against outside messages, yet sometimes we, the insiders, become traitors and sabotage ourselves. There were (and sometimes still are) moments when I was my own worst critic; I could beat anyone in a game of talking trash about myself.

Guilt, Shame, and Conviction

It is important for someone struggling with sexual addiction as well as the one who loves him to learn to distinguish between conviction, shame, and guilt. There are several reasons for this, but the most important is that guilt and shame are the primary drivers of acting out sexually. Referring to our previous chapter, these underlying, internal experiences are far more influential than the external world. But many people focus on the external world. Especially for wives, the source of their husbands' temptation seems to be body type, physique, age, hair color, or clothing. In reality, these things are secondary to the internal world. Let's first look at what is happening when we feel guilt, shame, and conviction and then connect how they inform struggles with sexual integrity.

Guilt

Guilt has gotten a bad rap. Pastors, helpers, counselors, and psychologists have differing views on what guilt is and does. For our conversation, let's simply describe guilt as an emotion we experience when we behave badly or do not behave well. Whether by conscience or by the Holy Spirit, we experience a sense that our choices and subsequent actions fall short or miss the mark. The guilty emotion is in place to motivate us to correct our behavior.

Think of guilt as a message to us that says, "I *made* a mistake." This statement is *behavior*-oriented, describing our actions and activities. It is not *being*-oriented. The message is neither a statement of value nor one of worth. Nothing in it indicates consequence or repercussion. Though both consequences and repercussions are certainly present in reality, guilt makes no declaration of these; it merely points to whether our actions align with our values. It is worth mentioning that for some people, the barometer of what should or should not produce guilt is out of calibration. A person's experiences and programming, especially in childhood, inform what is right or wrong, and that is woven into his value system. Add to that a faith background rooted more in rules than relationships, and this can tremendously distort someone's guilt meter. But whether or not the barometer is out of calibration, at some point, the guilt bleeds over into shame.

Shame

Shame is a difficult topic. Shame is a feeling and self-concept that is wholly fraudulent. It involves a deep core belief that we are defective and potentially broken beyond repair. As a follower of Christ and a believer in the Bible, you might be tempted to read the last sentence and think, "Yeah, we are defective and broken—it's called original sin!" But when we talk about shame, we aren't talking about brokenness with respect to our fallen humanity. Instead, shame deals with our sense of identity and worth.

Shame tells us that the cores of our souls, which God handcrafted, are broken to the point of worthlessness—that God made a mistake with us or that maybe we aren't worth saving. Shame may say that God has given up on us and others likely will too. Boil it down and the message of shame is a trifecta of pain. Here is the threefold message of shame:

1. I am worthless.
2. I am unlovable.
3. I am unforgivable.

Where guilt says, "I *made* a mistake," shame takes it a step further and says, "I *am* a mistake." It is an outright indictment of one's being—on who a person is and whose he is. These painful thought patterns and emotional experiences can be overwhelming and flat-out debilitating. They can make it hard to even get out of bed. And once we get up, it can feel like the world is out to prove just how worthless, unlovable, and unforgivable we are. On top of that, a spiritual war is waging within us—Satan enters the scene here to pile it on. The indictments can penetrate our hearts like a dagger: "You're a hypocrite," "You're a loser," "You don't deserve love," "Your family would be better off without you," "The world would be better off without you," "You're beyond hope," and "You're pathetic" are common refrains in the soul of someone struggling with shame. At the height of my shame, I could hardly look at myself in the mirror. When I did, I was riddled with disappointment and disdain for the man who was looking back at me.

It's a tragedy that these messages sink in so deeply to our souls, because Scripture specifically speaks to these faulty messages. Psalm 139:14 says, "I praise you because I am fearfully and wonderfully made." Within this verse, the word *fearfully* is the Hebrew word *yare'*, which refers to a deed performed in a wonderful manner, usually referring to God. The Hebrew word for *wonderful* used herein is *palah*, which means "distinguished, set apart, and admirable." In other words, God took delight in imagining us, designing us uniquely, creating us, and making us in His image. We are intrinsically valuable just by the very fact that God made us!

Shame Hangover

While shame can hit head on and be overwhelming emotionally, it also has a hangover effect. On the backside of getting slimed with shame's message, we may begin believing that the antidote is better behavior. There's a sense that we can somehow behave our way out of the indictment. If we can get over some arbitrary behavioral threshold, then we won't have to feel so bad about ourselves. Or if we've really performed well, then we'll have some credit that we can draw on when we're a little off the rails and feel sort of bad but not be completely overtaken by the shame. The unfortunate outcome is that it creates and reinforces a shame-induced, performance-based identity. The underlying faulty link is the notion that our beings are predicated on our behavior—that who we are is a function of what we do, not the other way around. When we live this way, we make matters worse by addressing the symptom instead of the problem. Instead of internalizing our worth, forgiveness, and love as a function of our existence in the mind of the Creator, we try to behave our way into being valuable human beings. I don't know about your life, but in mine, I can only white-knuckle good behavior for a short time. That's exactly why I need a Savior.

The confusing part about shame is that we know instinctively that we should feel bad for our behavior. The person who acts out sexually usually knows it is wrong and hurtful to him and those he loves. The problem is, this unhealthy, toxic shame is wrapped around the axle with an appropriate feeling of conviction.

Conviction

As we discussed shame, you might also have thought, "But the Bible talks about shame, so why is it a bad thing?" And you'd be right. The Bible does talk about shame, from cover to cover. For the sake of clarity, I'd like to make a distinction between terms. The shame we talked about in the last section we'll call *toxic shame*, and going forward, when we refer to the shame described in the

Bible, we'll call it *conviction*. Conviction penetrates our spirits, telling us we've sinned and thereby grieved the heart of God. It is not meant to make us feel like we're monsters; instead, it's intended to prompt repentance. That sense of conviction is designed to point out our unholiness, the state of our sanctification and how lacking it is compared to God's desire for us. It is meant to help us recognize the depravity of the fallen state of humanity, not make us feel worthless. For someone struggling with sexual integrity issues, conviction and shame are a tangled mess. It's nearly impossible to distinguish between the two. Like I said, most believers who struggle acknowledge that they should feel bad about their sins, but the bad feeling overwhelms them.

The best way for us to parse the experience is to identify the responses it prompts. Guilt, as an emotional response to behavior outside our values, prompts a change in behavior, not a change of heart. Shame, indicting one's being, prompts isolation and hiding. It perpetuates ways of coping that usually entail harmful habits. Of particular note is sexual acting out. When we feel shame, we don't want to see ourselves in the mirror or interact with the people we love, and we usually don't want to engage with God. Alternatively, conviction, which we now know is biblical shame, prompts repentance and a return to relationships. It drives us to acknowledge our depravity and need for a Savior, thus turning us from our sins and pushing us to lean into relationships. Conviction propels us to press into what God wants to do in our lives and allow Him to change our character, the by-product of which will be a change in behavior. Conviction points us toward true repentance, not just being sorry. Conviction banks on grace.

Origins of Shame

Overt

Remember the message of shame: you are unlovable, unforgivable, worthless. Shame has its roots in our life experiences, especially those from early childhood. Theoretically, a myriad of experiences might imprint the threefold message of shame. To narrow that list a bit, we can hone in on neglect, abuse, and abandonment.

Conceptually, it is not a stretch of the imagination to see that neglect might injure a child, whether that neglect is emotional, mental, spiritual, or physical. I talk often with men who grew up in a generation where having a roof, clothes, and three meals a day meant you were loved. *Emotional neglect* is not the label used to describe what they experienced, but that's what it truly may have been. The heart of that child wasn't nurtured, comforted, and loved. They never went hungry, but they were emotionally starved.

A similar dialogue can be had around abuse. What exactly is *abuse*? We can define it as a term: to treat (a person or an animal) with cruelty or violence, especially regularly or repeatedly. But what amounts to cruel treatment is very subjective. What hurts one child's heart may have little effect on another. There are also different types of abuse: spiritual, physical, sexual, mental, and emotional. What we define as *having been abused* is often a combination of several of these types.

The point here is that where there was abuse in someone's childhood experience, there are likely wounds of shame. When you look at it through the threefold-message framework, it makes sense. A six-year-old who was repeatedly told he was stupid, defective, and would never amount to anything did not have the faculties to process what he was hearing. What gets internalized is a message of worthlessness and unlovability. It's almost inevitable. A little girl who was repeatedly spanked to the point of bruises and welts did not have the framework to interpret the punishment. She didn't know that the punishment did not fit the crime. She didn't understand that it was because her father had anger issues and not because she was worthless. What she internalizes is the message that she is unforgivable.

As it pertains to abandonment, we have to remember that the experience is subject to interpretation by the person to whom it happened. Further, it can involve humans and God. Some people feel abandoned by a parent who leaves after a divorce, friends who move on, or family members who pass away. Likewise, it can feel like God has abandoned us when we lose these important figures in our lives.

A client told me that when his father left and married another woman, he felt abandoned by his dad. He became the black sheep among his new stepsiblings, and he was bullied and suffered physical abuse. As a child, his heart was scarred; he wondered why God would allow all this to happen to him. He felt abandoned by God. Here again, it was almost inevitable that messages of shame set in:

- "If God loved me, He wouldn't let this happen to me."
  —Unlovable
- "What have I done to deserve this?" —Unforgivable
- "If I meant anything to God, He would save me from this or put our family back together." —Worthless

Overt causes of shame typically can be categorized as those things that we would expect to harm the heart of a child. But there are also covert causes of shame.

Covert

To this point, I've tried to remind you of the idea that everyone's experience is unique. What wounds one person's heart may not affect another at all. Even within a family structure, what elicits shame in one child might be a nonissue for another. This is important to remember when dealing with covert causes of shame as well.

Covert causes are those experiences that bring on the threefold message of shame seemingly accidentally. There is no willful harm or ill intention involved. The damage done may be inadvertent, but it is damage nonetheless. One way this occurs is in the context of family rules. Statements such as "big boys don't cry" or "children are to be seen and not heard" can contribute to shame. An adult saying these things is usually well intentioned. The goal of "big boys don't cry" is to teach boys to toughen up and develop the resilience to deal with life's painful realities. "Children are to be seen and not heard" imparts a social norm: respect adults who are talking and learn how to appropriately interrupt a conversation, or be silent when the circumstances require it. Both are good things to learn. These are life skills. Yet they may cause inadvertent damage.

Think about an eleven-year-old who has heard "big boys don't cry" since he was two, month after month, year after year. Without the faculties to understand context—without additional explanation, teaching, and guidance—he might begin to believe that crying is effeminate. What is more, he might begin to internalize that to mean that showing emotion is bad or wrong. But he cannot reconcile that with the way some things tap into his heart and make the tears well up. So what is he to make of this message that clashes against his created design? Shame sets in. "What's wrong with me?" he might ask. He may question his manhood. Then the shame can start to warp his self-concept: if he is not manly, he might be a failure. He might be worthless or unlovable. Many men who struggle with sexual integrity issues have a story like this and end up fraudulently trying to affirm their masculinity through association with femininity. In other words, the more women he can get to want him, like him, or have sex with him, the more of a man he must be.

Another covert cause can be circumstantial. I have a client who was never physically abused, never abandoned, and never neglected in the strictest sense of the word. However, at five, his younger brother, then three years old, was diagnosed with a terminal illness. Most of the following several years of this man's childhood were spent in hospital waiting rooms. By no fault of his own, no ill intent on his parents' part, and no abusive dynamic involved, his heart was scarred. Those years of his childhood were lost, taking a backseat to the acute needs of his brother. Questions began to loom, like "Do I matter?" and "What about me?" His parents were doing everything they could to maintain the care his brother needed while still giving him attention and holding down jobs to pay mounting medical bills. His shame was nobody's fault. It had a covert cause.

In closing, it is important to remember that whether the source of shame is covert or overt, the consequence is the same: it wounds our hearts. In adulthood, those wounds get salt poured in them. Life happens: Our spouses get angry, causing us to question whether we're lovable. We fail at work or parenting, and we feel worthless. Sometimes we make mistakes that seem as though they cannot be forgiven—even by God. The salt in the wound stings and burns, and pain begins to mount. Anxiety increases, and we begin to look for an anesthetic, something to numb the pain. People who struggle with sexual integrity issues have learned how to use their sexuality as that painkiller.

Shelley's Thoughts

Watching Jason identify the wounds of his past—as well as the unhealthy ways he managed life up to that point—helped me understand the why *behind his sexual integrity issues. It certainly didn't excuse his behavior, but it did help explain how he landed where he landed and why he started to make the choices he did well before I met him. As he worked through these issues, he felt a greater sense of freedom and joy.*

Later on in our recovery, after I had worked through a lot of the pain and grief that Jason brought upon me, I felt compelled to look at my own past wounds. Jason's work motivated me, and I wanted to experience the same freedom and joy.

Something beautiful and unexpected came out of this work for me: a deeper empathy for Jason. As I began to recognize my wounds and grieve them, I was able to more fully see his wounds. I started to see him less as the man that broke my heart and more as the deeply hurt little boy who so badly wanted to be loved and accepted.

Little did I know then that Jason's journey would give me the courage to look within my heart for the wounds I was carrying around. Working on my past hurts and unhealthy ways of dealing with life and allowing God to change me cultivated in me an empathy for Jason that I never thought would be possible.

CHAPTER FOUR

The Internal World

I want to provide a little window into the mind of a sexual addict. I certainly can't speak for everyone who struggles with sexual sin, but because I have struggled personally and have helped other men as well, I can say that these are some common realities. My hope is to give anyone reading this a glimpse of these realities and to break down a common misconception. Some people think that for a sexually addicted person, it is all fun and games, with excitement and adventure as the preeminent experience. His ultimate desire is to pursue a playboy lifestyle, and he has only momentary breaches of guilt and shame. In fact, it is quite the opposite. The excitement and adventure are real but fleeting. The guilt, shame, and conviction are common and persistent, sometimes even unbearable, and they actually drive the person struggling to act out all over again. This chapter is my attempt to paint a more realistic picture and help explain that it is often more pain than pleasure.

Compartmentalization

I wrote about compartmentalization in *Worthy of Her Trust* using the metaphor of a closet full of boxes: one box contains all the things related to acting out, another contains home life, and yet another contains work life. There are rigid boundaries between them until those lines of distinction get broken down. That can happen accidentally or intentionally, but it is rarely planned.[7] What I mean is that, for example, visiting prostitutes may be a part of someone's acting-out pattern, but having an affair with a coworker is nowhere on the radar. And then, somewhere along the way, those lines get crossed and work becomes enveloped in the acting-out process. It wasn't planned, but it became yet another part of life swallowed up by the vortex of the addiction.

Rather than thinking of compartmentalization as entirely negative, remember that it was developed as a way of dealing or coping with life. In childhood, it may have helped make sense of the world when there was abuse, abandonment, neglect, or chaos. It started with survival. It resulted in a framework for life that is not integrated. It is disjointed, parsed, and piecemeal. The life, addiction, work, and hobbies boxes all have connecting aspects, but the framework was set up to keep things separate. For many people struggling with addiction, there are several consequences.

First, it makes transitions difficult. Moving from one box to another can cause anxiety, anger, or a feeling of being overwhelmed, especially when moving from a negative space like the acting-out box into positive space like the home-life box. When the addictive tendencies are activated and preoccupation or ritualistic activities are engaged, to interrupt them and transition can instigate intense anger. Wives will report that their husbands respond with rage when they change plans or rearrange activities. After learning about the addiction, they can see in retrospect that most plan changes interrupted the addictive cycle. Sometimes it's because the wife ended up being home when the original plan was that she would be gone or because the husband needed to be on call for kid duties instead of having the evening free.

The person struggling might feel entitled and selfish about parts of his life that feel more personal if he is compartmentalizing. When other people have to be involved—like his wife, for instance—there can be a ton of friction. The person struggling may draw lines around what belongs to him: his car, his radio settings, his basement. He gets to control what show is on television. He gets to decide how to spend his free time, often regardless of whom it inconveniences. He is also protective and secretive about his personal things. Typically, this pertains to gym bags, wallets, desks, glove boxes or consoles, junk drawers, phones, computers, and so on.

This disintegrated framework precludes unity within the marital relationship. I would get anxious and uncomfortable if Shelley wanted to see my wallet, was on my computer, or was looking in a junk drawer of mine. That was true even when I knew I had nothing to hide at that moment. I wasn't afraid of getting caught—it was just mine! Today, Shelley has full access to anything of mine at any time. She can look at my wallet, phone, computer, or rummage through my car all she wants. *They belong to her too*—they aren't just mine. No compartments.

The compartmentalization often exacerbates disjointed thinking too. It comes off as selfish, but it is simply a function of the old survival framework. To block out one area while being involved in another was a useful skill at one point. Only now, the application of the skill is detrimental because it leads to self-centeredness.

While at work, thinking about what is happening at home is usually distant or nonexistent—unless, of course, it is involved in the acting-out process (when someone will or won't be home, for example). But that disjointed thinking extends into all areas of life. It means that when the addictive box is activated, its impact on other areas of life gets downplayed or disregarded.

Our big-picture, long-term goal in recovery is not just selflessness or to stop acting out. In fact, it is better characterized as holistic integration. We want the boxes to be broken down, the rigid boundaries to be softened, and to be the same person inside and out in whatever situation we find ourselves.

Crisis of Identity

Another aspect of living inside the addiction is a crisis of identity. There is a tension that develops this way: I know who I am, yet I don't like who I am, and I know who I want to be, and I see glimpses of that person, but I default to who I don't want to be, and sometimes I wonder if maybe I really am that person, not the person I thought myself to be. Confusing, right? It is an existential identity crisis. Such is life inside the mind of someone with an addiction.

If anyone can track with Paul and the book of Romans, it is someone struggling with addiction. Romans 7 says it all, and it's summed up in verses 21 and 22: "So I find this law at work: Although I want to do good, evil is right there with me. For in my inner being I delight in God's law, but I see another law at work in me, waging war against the law of my mind and making me a prisoner of the law of sin at work within me."

The identity crisis is further confused by shame. Remember that shame is an indictment of a person's being, an incriminating and invalidating statement about who he is. When he lives into the messages of shame, they are confirmed. Every episode of acting out and each level of escalation can feel like another chasm between who he thought he was and who he thinks he really is. For the person struggling with addiction, the repetitive nature of his acting out serves as the final confirmation of this—a stamp of defectiveness. He begins to believe he is what he's become.

When this is combined with the compartmentalization, duplicity begins to develop. For some struggling, the duplicity manifests between work and home or church and home. If you polled the audience of coworkers or fellow church volunteers, they would list off the great qualities and character traits of that person. They would report how generous, thoughtful, caring, patient, and so on the addict is. The external presentation to those people really isn't a show or manipulation; it is typically sincere. The rub, however, is that the identity crisis inside the addict is driving the external presentation.

For me, the worse I felt about myself, the more I tried to make up for it with the way I presented externally. Having binged over the weekend, I was more likely to be super caring to people at work, especially toward women, in my case. When I acted out on the road, I would sometimes return home and try to get the best husband award from Shelley by helping around the house. But the dissonance continued to grow until finally I surrendered to the idea that I really was the sum total of my behaviors and my value was tied to my actions. Eventually, the external started to line up with the internal, and I became increasingly rude and disrespectful to Shelley, clients, bosses, people in traffic, the grocery store checkout clerk, and everyone else. I began living into who I had become, not who I really was.

This whole dynamic is both scary and infuriating for wives because they never know who they're going to get. They just don't know who will walk in the door at 5:30 p.m. today. There is internal confusion because most wives believe their husbands to be caring, loving, patient, serving, and gentle people deep down. But wives then begin to doubt their own internal radar because they consistently experience their husbands as angry, entitled, arrogant, selfish, or disengaged.

My bias on this crisis is that, ultimately, God is wooing the authentic identity out. The "old man" that Paul talks about in his epistles is dying a slow, painful death (Rom. 6:6). Yet the implications of the addictive life infiltrate the ways of the new man still.

Chaos

The internal world for a person struggling with sexual addiction is chaotic. There is little peace and often a feeling of impending crisis. Previously, I described acting out as an intoxicating anesthetic; one aspect of the drug is that it briefly calms the chaos.

The chaos for me became something of a constant. It permeated my thinking and corresponding behavior. For example, it perpetuated my indecisiveness. I had a difficult time making decisions at work; I felt paralyzed by the possible bad outcomes and how they would reflect poorly on me. In retrospect, I can see that was informed by shame; I didn't want to confirm externally the way I felt about myself internally. The indecisiveness showed up at home, where, when making decisions about paint colors, decorating, activities, and so on, I would default to whatever Shelley wanted. Then, when I did disagree or have a counter opinion, I would avoid the conflict, stuff my feelings down, and harbor resentment toward her. That, in turn, created relational chaos. There was nearly constant relational ambiguity: I never knew where I stood with her. I would judge that we were okay by the fact that we weren't fighting. In other words, the absence of conflict was intimacy to me. That's a poor definition of connection and intimacy!

The chaos also creates a sense of restlessness. Many men I work with experience the feeling that they should be busy, always doing something—if nothing meaningful, then at least puttering. This kind of nervous anxiety drives some to be high achievers. Always thinking about the next idea or the next business venture or hobby nearly becomes an addiction in itself! Unfortunately, that restlessness also drives acting out. It is self-perpetuating. Within the addiction, we know that being bored is a dangerous thing. Yet staying busy is not necessarily healthy either. In addition, for many, being bored comes with a sense of worthlessness and insignificance. Sort of like, "If I have nothing to do, then I have no worth," although it's typically not expressly stated. In the space of boredom, acting out helps some people cope with the worthlessness. But this is followed by another onslaught of guilt and shame, which leads to busyness to avoid thinking about it and feeling it. The vicious cycle is chaos.

Corrosion

Within the inner workings of the person struggling with sexual addiction, there is corruption, if you will, of heart and mind. Let's look at these separately, and then we'll see how they work in conjunction.

As it pertains to the heart, some people would suggest the issue is a lack of one! Some wives will say that a man must be heartless to behave this way. That is not the case. Another way of saying it is that the person is bad—he's just a wicked or evil man. That is not the case either, in my opinion. I tend toward metaphors and analogies, and another one fits here.

The heart of a man who commits sexual sin is one that is corroded. Think of the heart like a car battery. There is a connection between the cable and the node. That link, if broken, prevents the battery from performing its primary job—providing an electric current to the engine. Without it, the engine won't start. Sure, you can jump it, but that's temporary and lasts only the duration of the current trip. Sometimes the link isn't broken completely, thus the electrical system will still work—you can turn on your lights and radio when the car isn't running, but there won't be enough juice to start the engine. When the battery node and the cable connector corrode, the link is lost. Where once it was a shiny, metal-on-metal connection, now it is crusty and discolored with caked-on turquoise and off-white powder. If it gets really bad, you can't even see the node or the connector—it is just one big clod of crud. *Clod* and *crud*: those are technical terms in Oklahoma, where I grew up. Anyway, that's what the heart looks like when it's corroded by sin.

Removing the corrosion is a painful and messy process. You have to scrape, hammer, chisel, and file. You use multiple tools, and you may need to spray it with gunk remover or even pour Coca-Cola on it! Then you rinse and repeat until there is solid contact again. It's no easy task. But when it's finished and filed clean, the connection is reestablished, and the battery provides the necessary current to jump-start the engine. The same is true of the heart.

Over time, with repeated violations of conscience and sins, the heart begins to corrode. It becomes coated in crud. That coating keeps the person from feeling the intensity of his own pain and also limits his ability to empathize with others' pain. It numbs his conscience to the consequence of his sin and results in disconnecting him from God—in other words, he is not getting any current from the source. For things to change, he has to wash away the corrosion. He must scrape and file to reestablish the connection.

That process is biblically known as progressive sanctification. The process is facilitated by humility within the body of Christ in the context of community. This is exactly what is described in Proverbs 27:17: "As iron sharpens iron, so one person sharpens another." That loud, clanging, sharp, hot, shrapnel-flinging process is sanctification happening. It is painful. Yet as the corrosion is removed, the heart starts to soften. The person can feel again. He begins to sense other people's pain. He begins to see the world as Jesus saw the world, and his heart breaks as His did.

By the way, I know every metaphor breaks down, and this one does as well: at some point, you just replace the old battery. That's not so easy with your own heart or with your husband's!

Conscience

Along with the heart issue, there is an issue in the mind. There is a conscience issue. *Conscience* is used in a couple different ways biblically, and for this conversation, I am referring to a particular usage: the soul distinguishing between what is morally good and bad, prompting you to do the former and shun the latter, commending the one, condemning the other. When someone is addicted, he does not lose the ability to distinguish between right and wrong morally, but he becomes desensitized to his soul when it commends or condemns behaviors. Habitual and repetitive sins, in practice, become almost ingrained. If we were talking sports, we would discuss biomechanics and muscle memory: the muscles become accustomed to—or, in a sense, "learn"—to follow the same fluid motion. In a similar fashion, the more a person violates his conscience, ignores the conviction of the Holy Spirit, and disobeys God's directions, the easier it becomes to do so. Additionally, when you factor in the neural chemistry of dopamine and the brain's reward system, you have a recipe for repetitive sin.

The two work in conjunction with each other; when you violate your conscience, you drain your compassion tank. You reduce your ability to practice empathy and be tender, gentle, and humble. When you violate your conscience, you're thumbing your nose at the prompting of the Holy Spirit. You're essentially saying to God, "I know what You say I should do and how I should live, but no thanks, I'm going to do my own thing." That taps into conviction, which it should. But as we've discussed, conviction is wrapped around the axle with shame, and once shame gets activated, self-protection kicks in. I can't feel someone else's pain if my energy is being used to protect myself from feeling my own pain!

To recap, the internal world of the person struggling with sexual integrity issues is rarely characterized by calm and clear thinking. It is frequently chaotic. Compartmentalization provides relief by insulating the person from having to bear the full weight of sin. His heart is corroded, and it often has been for years. This is scary when we understand biblically that the heart is the wellspring of life and should be protected at all costs (Prov. 4:23). It is the epicenter of values and morals. Additionally, the struggler's conscience is dulled, making it increasingly difficult for him to make sound decisions. He becomes disillusioned with truth and begins to believe his own lies. I say this not to excuse the harmful behaviors but to explain in a small way what is happening internally.

Shelley's Thoughts

I love the car battery analogy; I don't know that I appreciated the depth of Jason's corrosion at the beginning of our healing journey. As Jason mentioned, not only do we not know which version of our husbands we are going to get when they walk in the door before discovery or disclosure, but we also don't know which version of our husbands we might get during the first months/years of their recovery. The internal struggle going on within our husbands is no joke, and I quickly found that I was the one pouring on the Coca-Cola! What that means is that I was expecting a change and not settling for anything less. I would often insist on things I needed to see change and ways I wanted him to be different. Splashing Coke on the battery meant there was fizzing and bubbling, but that only loosened the crud a bit. It turns out that the deeper work of scraping and filing was best left to God, our counselor, and Jason's accountability partners.

This makes for an incredibly messy process. If you think for a moment this will be easy or squeaky-clean, think again. Yet I now know that the less-than-glamorous, not-so-glitzy first couple of years of our process actually laid the foundation for the years that followed.

CHAPTER FIVE

Impact on the Spouse

In this section, I'd like to take time to explain the experience of many wives during this process. I also want to answer some of the key questions that arise for wives once the truth is out. Whether uncovered by disclosure or, more often, discovery, the confusion and ensuing tumult wreak havoc on a wife. It can feel like you are losing yourself, being swallowed up by the tidal wave of crazy emotions and untamed thoughts. Some of the questions that loom are unanswerable, and anything that might explain what has happened usually feels more like an excuse. Yet understanding *why* is important—not because an academic explanation makes the pain go away, but simply because it gives some semblance of sense to something so senseless. Hopefully, this section will give you some handholds for when it feels like a free fall. To begin, we'll look at how your personal story informs your reaction to sexual betrayal.

Your Story

First, let's consider your personal story and past. Beginning with childhood, were you affected by infidelity within your family unit? If so, there is undoubtedly residue. It may not be something you deal with every day, but what happened left an imprint or narrative in you. Whoever was involved in the betrayal is important too. If it was Mom, it can inform your ideas of women—from their trustworthiness to expectations of how a woman behaves in the wake of discovery. How Dad handled the situation can also leave a mark. If it was Dad who committed the offense, it can influence your perception of what is permissible for men as well as your level of trust for men. If it didn't happen in your immediate family but instead with someone in your extended family, there are norms (often unintentionally) defined by what happened and how the issue got discussed. This can contribute to a future open dialogue or a staunch commitment to keeping secrets. The point here is that what went on in childhood, relative to fidelity and sexual integrity, informs the way we experience those things today.

The narrative or imprint can also be informed by a person's early or adolescent sexual experiences. These can range from playing doctor and experimenting sexually to childhood sexual abuse or rape. Much like our conversation about shame for sexual addicts, a person may still feel the residue of shame from these experiences. Later, when sexual betrayal becomes a part of her story in marriage, the nerves of that old shame get pricked, and the emotions of those previous experiences come rushing back. This can make the restoration process more difficult, and for some wives, it can require more intensive counseling help.

Someone who never experienced sexual betrayal will be familiar with an altogether different narrative. I've talked to women who, by the time they left home, never knew a family struck with betrayal. That doesn't mean that it didn't happen, but perhaps it was never public. The concept of infidelity, sexual acting out, or sexual immorality of any sort was completely foreign. You can imagine that, as an adult, experiencing betrayal firsthand defies categories for this person.

Reflection

Think back to when you were between six and sixteen years old. What memories come to mind regarding sexuality, experimentation, fidelity, or infidelity? Was there sexual betrayal in your immediate family or in your extended family? What was its impact on you? Do you remember the point of impact—when you found out? Do you remember the emotions associated with the experiences? Are the memories and emotions fresh or are they distant? Your answers to these questions will inform the way you experience your own betrayal. The narrative or imprint resident inside you will accentuate or dull your emotions, reactions, and thought processes.

Now we'll move on to those experiences beyond childhood that impact the way we experience betrayal. Consider your romantic life, beginning back when you first started dating. For some women, those early years discovering boys were exciting and adventurous, and the memories are fond. They have an overarching theme of being chosen and pursued. For other women, the memories are filled with pain. They are characterized by rejection, and the pain of heartbreak and betrayal even in dating is still acute. For others, the memories are blank. There was no dating. Ranging from religious beliefs to developmental reasons, boys never were a thing. Dating, dances, first kisses, and especially first sexual encounters weren't highlights—they were no-lights! Whichever the case, each has its own imprint or narrative. These early dating experiences (or the lack thereof) often, unfortunately, result in faulty core beliefs about oneself. This can be the origin point, or the confirmation point, of negative self-concept statements like these:

- I'm ugly.
- I'm dumb.
- I'm loved for my body, not my heart.
- My *no* means *yes*.
- My voice doesn't matter.
- My value is a function of my weight.

The point here is that these faulty core beliefs will still be resident in you as an adult and thus incorporated into your marriage. As you can imagine, sexual betrayal does a number on these beliefs, further engraining them into one's consciousness.

In my opinion, this is the most acute, most insidious, most tragic damage done by sexual betrayal. As husbands, we are called to create a space where our wives' deepest hurts and the most scarring wounds on their souls can be healed, covered, smoothed, and renewed. Ephesians 5:25–27 tells us this: "Husbands, love your wives, just as Christ loved the church and gave himself up for her to make her holy, cleansing her by the washing with water through the word, and to present her to himself as a radiant church, without stain or wrinkle or any other blemish, but holy and blameless."

In other words, those faulty core beliefs should become null and void and be replaced with the God-given truth about her identity. Instead, betrayal accomplishes nearly the exact opposite.

Moving on, the final data points as they pertain to your story are borne out by your romantic history in adulthood. My heart breaks for wives I talk to who married later in life, primarily putting it off due to fear. Then, somewhere along the way, they decided to take the plunge and now feel like they're getting punished for it. I hate that. If that's your story, on behalf of the man you waited for who disappointed you, I am so sorry.

The same goes for the woman who has landed on her third or fourth iteration of marriage, begging for it finally to be different. When I hear the story of how her first marriage ended due to sexual betrayal, I cringe because it seems as though the script is prewritten and predestined. You almost know the ending in advance.

Some of the wives I talk to never took the time to figure out why they were drawn to men with sexual integrity issues. It seems as though a lot of people in the helping field like to point that out. "Well, she hasn't done her work," they'll say. We helpers sometimes say the dumbest things. I'm sorry. And frankly, many women *have* done their work! And they thought they were in the clear this time, only to be duped by a man who didn't tell the truth on the front side of her changing her last name again. I hate that too, mainly because that's what I did to Shelley. I lied and downplayed my issues on the front end and manipulated her into saying yes to my proposal, then backed her into a corner to follow through on the big Texas wedding. Anyway, the experiences of prior marriages will have an impact on how sexual betrayal impacts you.

Ultimately, you are currently living the sum total of your story. Who you are is not the sum total of your story—you are more than that. But the influence of these past experiences has a cumulative effect on our emotions, thought patterns, and souls. The narrative or imprint creates a schematic through which present-day information is processed. Thus the impact of sexual betrayal today will elicit a reaction based on this processing. What that looks like can be surprising, confusing, and overwhelming. You may find yourself thinking, doing, and saying things you didn't know you were capable of. On the flip side of the coin, you may find yourself functioning as a fighter and survivor, dealing with pain in ways you also didn't know you were capable of. It is both tragic and beautiful at the same time. In fact, we'll talk more about this in a later chapter.

For now, suffice it to say that past wounds and imprints, combined with present-day betrayal, land wives on a roller coaster ride they never intended to buy a ticket for. That roller coaster is called "grieving."

Grieving

As soon as a wife finds out what is happening, she begins to grieve. Typically, we think of grieving as associated with the death of a person. In this case, however, the death is that of an ideal and a perceived reality. Much the same way someone might grieve the loss of a close friend or relative, a wife grieves the loss of her marriage, its fidelity, and the concept she had of her husband and herself. Think of grieving as a way of making sense of your story. At the Every Man's Battle workshops, I describe the grieving process as a giant jigsaw puzzle. A wife's life is like a ten-thousand-piece puzzle, glued and framed. When disclosure and/or discovery happens, it's as if her husband is taking a baseball bat, rearing back, and swinging at it like it's a fastball. When the bat meets the frame, the whole puzzle shatters, sending the pieces flying all over the place. Then the wife, trying to make sense of her life, attempts to fit the pieces back together, wondering what the real picture was all along, because it sure wasn't what she thought it was. Running with the metaphor, think about how you do a puzzle. What do you do first? Before you can even do the edges or corners, before you can group like pieces together, you have to turn them all over, face up. You have to know what pieces you're dealing with. Such is the case for wives after discovery/disclosure.

That process of making sense of the story happens in stages. Elizabeth Kubler Ross is recognized as having identified the five stages of grief. You've probably heard of them:

1. denial
2. anger
3. bargaining
4. hopelessness
5. resolution

Denial and resolution are fairly self-explanatory. The three middle stages are the ones I want to give a little detail on because they have a tremendous impact on how a wife engages with her husband.

Anger

The anger stage can be confusing for a wife. If you are accustomed to being angry, then it comes naturally, and this stage may not look much different than other times of conflict. If you are a "stuffer," "avoider," or generally have lived believing anger is wrong or bad, then this stage may surprise you. But the anger is important. Remember that righteous anger is a right response to injustice. Betrayal is an injustice. I encourage wives to get angry and, if they need to, yell, scream, and throw heavy things in their husbands' general direction. Remember those mashed potatoes at Christmas dinner? This is when those would fly. Now, I'm not advocating physical violence, but I am encouraging a wife to get in touch with that deep righteous anger. The Bible clearly tells us there is a line to it: "In your anger do not sin" (Eph. 4:26). But where is that line? As a wife, you'll need to do business with Jesus to figure out where that line is. In my experience, when that anger isn't actualized, it gets stuffed into a vault, then decays into resentment and bitterness that seeps out over decades. Nobody wants that. So it is important to express your anger and get it out of you. Do that with your husband, with a friend or family member, your journal, or just by yelling when you're in your car alone. Get it out of you however you can.

Two cautions will counterbalance this permission to express the anger fully. First, it is important to remember that your husband is not the enemy or villain. It can feel that way, especially when he pops off in the middle of your anger and says something hurtful, accusatory, minimizing, or disrespectful. But he is not the enemy. He is still your husband, and there is still a person in pain standing in front of you—remember our discussion of the hurt kid inside of him. Please understand that I'm not trying to excuse or minimize his actions. I'm not trying to negate the pain you've been caused. I do, however, want you to see him for who he is, not all the bad things he's done. Too often, I see wives do their own damage when they hit the anger stage. They later feel their own shame and guilt and regret what they've done and said. You needn't add to your own pain.

The second caution relates to the details of your husband's acting out. For some wives, when the anger escalates, the intensity of questioning does as well. The questions become more detailed, more specific, and, frankly, more vulgar. I've had wives say they feel like they can't help themselves. When they hit that critical mass of anger, they aren't thinking straight, and there's a sense that every detail will somehow explain their husbands' behaviors. It feels like the explanation will make the pain end. It won't! It will only exacerbate it! Some of those details will never get erased. Further, your husband doesn't want to relive those details—if he does, then he's not ready to change. But more than likely, he's trying and praying for God to get that junk out of his head too. In the heat of the moment, when a wife digs into those nitty-gritty details of positions, pictures, color of clothing, the words said, the physical features, and so on, it can tap into his shame. Once that shame button gets pushed, self-preservation kicks in, and empathy wanes.

Once again, this is the exact opposite of what a wife desires and needs in those moments.

So how much anger is too much, and how much detail crosses the line? Honestly, there is no easy answer. And I think it is important for you to have permission to not know where the lines are. The truth is, you'll swing the pendulum on both of these. You'll scream and say things you regret, and the Holy Spirit will stir your spirit to feel conviction because it was over the line. But you'll be mindful of that line in the next go-round. You'll ask questions that you wish you hadn't gotten the answers to, but you'll be more attuned to it the next time you are in the heat of the moment. To put restrictions on what you ask or how you express your pain beyond the explicit guidelines of the Scriptures is to potentially limit your healing process. That said, we'll cover this more thoroughly later.

Bargaining

The bargaining phase is a confusing one for everyone involved. This stage functions as a buffer in many ways, taking the edge off the intensity of the anger and simultaneously staving off the depths of hopelessness. Think of bargaining as navigating the range of options available to find a sense of peace and stability and feel grounded. Granted, seeking these things is normal and good, and every wife going through this process wants them. The nuance here is that in the bargaining stage, the pursuit of those things can move from being a methodical, intentional, and healthy search into a knee-jerk reaction—one with lasting consequences that can interrupt or slow the healing process.

Wives bargain with several entities. They bargain with themselves, their husbands, their kids, their friends, and even God. I've heard wives say they made a deal with God that they will stick around until the kids go off to college, but then they are committed to divorcing. And it's not uncommon to hear a wife say she's praying to be released from the marriage but doesn't feel like God is giving her permission—*yet*.

I talk to so many wives who end up exhausted from the mental gymnastics. Some of this bargaining for their own sense of stability is juxtaposed against what is genuinely in the best interest of their husbands. Here's an example of what I'll hear when I talk to a wife about this:

I think I should kick him out. I need the space. I can't even think when I'm in the same room with him. Our kids can feel the tension, and it's getting increasingly awkward. He should stay somewhere else. But we can't afford two mortgages right now. And I don't want him in a hotel room. And I don't want him at some friend's house either; this is a private issue, and I don't want rumors started. And who knows what he'll do when he is out of the house—he might act out again. Maybe I'll just insist he move into the basement. Then at least I know what he's up to. But maybe I should kick him out; he needs the consequence. He needs to know living this way is not okay. No, he can just stay in our room. I'll move out. Let him see what it's like to sleep in our bed alone. Perhaps I'll just stay in the guest room. That way, we can still work on our marriage and try to heal. I don't know. It's too confusing for me to know what the right thing to do is.

You see the back and forth of this monologue? It is such a normal part of the process. You're not crazy. Wives struggle to figure out what is best for themselves, for their kids, and for their husbands. Sometimes wives want to punish their husbands and make them feel the same pain; sometimes they want their husbands to just "get" how much it hurts to be betrayed.

When you're in the bargaining stage, there are a couple of important guidelines to remember. First, *big decisions are not the best decisions* to make at this time. In the search for stability, making massive shifts runs counter to the desired outcome. Deciding on a separation or divorce, selling the house and moving across town or to a different state, pulling the kids out of school or enrolling them to a new one, selling vehicles, and shuffling large amounts of money around are examples of big decisions. Certainly, some circumstances require major movements. Sometimes you need to move money to be financially okay in light of his actions. Perhaps you need to leave for a while and take the kids to be with your folks in another state. Maybe making a job change is imperative. However, doing any of these things in knee-jerk fashion will likely give you more work to do or more of a mess to clean up later. Be sure that any major decisions you're making are run through the filter of your close friends and support system as well as your counselor. You want to move swiftly but not recklessly or irresponsibly.

Second, remember that *this is a stage and it will pass.* The way you feel this week and the intensity with which you insist on some boundaries will probably change by next month. You don't want to react out of fear, anxiety, and a sense of being overwhelmed only to regret those decisions in a few weeks. This is a consistent theme in my office. A wife will come in one week screaming mad, demanding I cosign on him moving out. I'll urge her to tap the brakes and find a similar but less severe solution, such as moving him into the basement. A couple weeks later, in a calmer, clearer mental state, that same wife will say she is glad for the space that his moving out of their bedroom created but also glad he's within earshot when she needs something.

As the bargaining stage dwindles, it gives way to the darkest part of the process, the hopelessness.

Hopelessness

This stage stinks. I hate it. Yet it is a necessary part of the healing process. The worst part about it, I think, is that it feels like all the work up to this point has been wasted. It seems as if everything is back at square one. Usually, that is not actually the case; it just feels that way because of the deep sadness that is setting in.

I would say the hopelessness stage for betrayed wives seems to be best characterized by regret. During this stage, they begin to reprocess years of memories that they thought were water under the bridge—whether just a few or several decades. They replay history: the comments made at the proposal dinner, the early marriage conflicts, or the general state of things prior to everything hitting the fan. The regret surrounds the circumstances as well as their personal choices and character flaws. During this internal processing, they second-guess themselves all over again and feel duped, stupid, foolish, or ridiculous, and it can be harder than ever to get out of bed.

The largest looming question is "Why?" Why did this happen? Why didn't God stop it? Why didn't I see it sooner? Why did I put up with it so long? Why go through any more pain? That last question can, for some wives, even lead to suicidal thoughts. These thoughts usually don't involve a plan of action, but they can include statements about escaping the pain inadvertently. I don't typically hear "I want to kill myself" so much as "I wouldn't mind if a semitruck swerved into my lane." My heart breaks when I hear wives talking this way, partly because I know they are almost there, nearly done with this painful journey. They are just about to cross over onto steady ground and sure footing. If you've had or are having these thoughts, please tell someone. Tell your best friend or your mom, whoever is safest. It would be good for your husband to know too, but he may not be safe enough to handle it today. Someone needs to know.

My advice for this stage is for wives to give themselves permission to practice self-care and hang on a little longer. You're almost there! Give yourself permission to ask for what you need. That may mean you need a pass on parenting and going to the kids' ball games and cheer practices. You might need to take some days off work; be okay with calling in sick, even if that seems to go against your work ethic. Or perhaps you need to build a house cleaner into the budget because cleaning and dusting aren't worth getting out of bed for today, but you'll also feel chaotic if the house isn't clean.

You may need to tweak the boundaries you previously set. Instead of him being in the basement, you may want him in the bed. Instead of not talking after nine o'clock at night, you may want to be able to talk anytime. Instead of him not bringing anything up, you may demand he ask how you're doing every evening.

This is also a time to practice self-care. It is time to schedule the massage or get that pedicure. You might need to let yourself off the hook from the strict diet. Maybe you could read a book rather than going to the gym today. During this stage, it can feel like the joy has been sucked out of everything and nothing is worth doing. But you are worth it. You are worth taking care of, so take care of yourself.

Shelley's Thoughts

Some of you might feel like practicing self-care is self-centered. It might make you feel uncomfortable to love yourself in this way. Others might be game for practicing some self-care but have no idea where to even start. Let's talk about these points a bit further.

If you feel like practicing self-care is selfish, I encourage you to think through why you feel this way. For instance, what did your caregivers model for you in this area growing up? If you had a mom who frowned on taking breaks from mothering or from work to do something she enjoyed, this might be informing your belief that self-care is selfish. Likewise, if, as a child, you didn't see your parents spending their money on anything other than necessities, this could be informing your opinion. Think through why you feel this way and then keep reading.

Not knowing where to start when it comes to practicing self-care is normal. It takes time and intentionality to figure out what makes us thrive, what brings us joy, what fills us up when we are empty. Below is a list of questions you can ask yourself in order to figure out what might help you meet your self-care needs:

- *What activities deplete me? What activities fill me up?*
- *What is helping me survive the day?*
- *What helps me feel comfortable? What helps me feel grounded?*
- *What am I passionate about?*

Once you take time to explore these questions, you should start to see some areas where you can practice self-care. For instance, in the winter, I love eating warm soups, wearing comfy pants, and curling up in a blanket with a good book. I'm passionate about living simply and not having a lot of clutter in my house. I'm also passionate about getting outside and exercising. I feel more grounded when (and this might seem strange to you) the beds are made. With that said, if I want to engage in self-care, I might go for a run. Or I might set the timer for fifteen minutes and pick up a certain room in my house and then treat myself to a small window of time spent reading. Or maybe I will put on my comfy pants and then pull out one of my favorite homemade soup recipes and prepare it for dinner.

Every day, it's important to do not one, not two, but several things in order to love yourself well. As you can see, it doesn't necessarily have to cost anything (making beds, anyone?) and it doesn't have to be time consuming (reading a good book for fifteen minutes). Remember, you are worth it!

In addition to giving themselves permission to practice self-care, I urge wives to be patient at this stage. Sometimes it lasts a few days, sometimes a few months. Ugh, I know. It can seem as if more of your life is being wasted on this process. But the fabric of your character and your walk with Christ are both being shaped and woven here. You are persevering. You are experiencing long-suffering, as much as that stinks and even though you were forced into it. In the end, you'll be a stronger version of yourself: you'll be more resilient but not hardened, more patient but not bitter, wiser but not at the expense of your sanity. This is the place where I think two sections of scripture come into sharp focus.

The first is Second Corinthians 12:9: His grace is sufficient, and His power is made perfect in our weakness. He will sustain you through this time. The second is First Corinthians 10:13: God will not let you be tempted beyond what you can handle, and when the going gets rough, when you're overwhelmed, He'll see you through it. We often think of temptation in this verse as some overt sexual sin or immorality. But the temptation can simply be to pull the ripcord on your marriage, even when you have biblical foundation to do so. He won't let you be crushed under the weight of it all; He'll walk with you. With His power and the empowerment of the Body of Christ alongside you, you'll get through it.

A Note for Husbands

These stages—anger, bargaining, and hopelessness—can make a wife feel crazy. They can make her feel like she is literally losing her mind. Likewise, they can feel crazy to you. But please, whatever you do, don't call her crazy! When you're traveling with her through the ups and downs emotionally, the tendency can be to default to logic and reasoning. But that's not usually helpful. You can't talk her out of her feelings. And trying to reason with her won't make the weight of the emotions lift—at least, not in the long run.

In addition, it can feel like the goalpost keeps moving. What she wanted or needed last week is different this week, and the rules of yesterday no longer apply. There was a set of parameters within which to operate, but just when you feel like you've got your head around them, they change. This is normal! Don't freak out. And don't allow yourself to begin thinking she is trying to create a trap for you to get caught in so that you fail. She's not. In fact, she probably hates the roller coaster more than you do. She doesn't like waking up wondering how she'll survive today any more than you do.

So be patient. Be proactive with empathy. Be considerate and kind. Take up the slack. Give her permission to grieve and make sense of her story. Serve till it hurts. Lean on your brothers for encouragement and support. Lean on God. Remember that you are a conduit of healing when you patiently walk with her and support her process of grieving.

Catastrophizing and Overgeneralizing

I'm not sure *catastrophizing* is a word. It may be another one I made up. But the root of it is a real word—*catastrophe*. The idea here is that in the heat and emotion of betrayal, there can be a tendency to see only the totality of the damage. *Overgeneralizations* in this sense are statements typically used to characterize the level of pain rather than accuse or increase the breadth of sin. It is not uncommon for wives who are in this place to paint with broad strokes what has happened and what has been tainted. These are some common statements I hear:

- All twenty-eight years of our marriage have been a waste!
- You've slept with every woman in the church!
- You've looked at every kind of porn out there.
- You're the worst husband on the planet.
- You've done nothing but lie to me since day one.

If you find yourself sitting in this pain, reflecting on how much has been lost due to sexual betrayal, remember that it's okay to grieve. However, if you find yourself ruminating on the totality of it to the point that you can't see through the fog to find much of anything good, remember that you are in the trenches of emotion and it won't always be this way. Further, as we previously discussed, the period when you are in the midst of that overwhelming sense of loss is not the time to make any major decisions. If you are feeling like every day of the last three decades was a waste, then it is easier to justify divorce as an outcome. However, if you can see through the catastrophizing, albeit dimly, you will probably be able to find truly foundational, meaningful aspects of the relationship. Perhaps it has to do with your ministry together, the kids, the trials you've been through with family illness, or your extended family.

Ultimately, you may not land there. In the end, you may decide that there truly was nothing to begin with. I don't want that outcome for you. I don't think that will be the outcome for you. But at least wait until you are out of the trench to make that decision.

CHAPTER SIX

Steps toward Healing

It's Not Your Fault

If you are like most, then when you find out your spouse has betrayed you sexually, you will have moments of self-doubt, questioning what you did or failed to do to cause it. The truth is that you did … nothing. If your spouse has been struggling with sexual integrity issues, it has absolutely nothing to do with you. It is not because of you or in spite of you. It has nothing to do with your body, your heart, your character, your flaws, your parenting, your faith journey—nothing. And it has nothing to do with how you play your role as a spouse. Whether you're doing everything wrong and contributing to a terrible marriage or everything right and creating the best possible environment, it doesn't make a difference either way.

What's Love Got to Do with It?

As terribly difficult as it is to understand, what your spouse has done has nothing to do with whether they love you. I wrote about this in *Worthy of Her Trust*, specifically as it pertains to men who act out sexually:

As counterintuitive as it may seem, men rarely commit sexual betrayal because of a lack or loss of love for their wife. Hardly ever does a man who has fallen sexually sit in my office and say that he doesn't love his wife anymore. It happens on occasion, but even then, it often is not true anyway. Usually when a husband expresses that he doesn't love his wife he is making a statement about his own shame. He is grasping at straws trying to make sense of his own behavior. The logic says, "If I am willing to hurt her this bad, over and over again, then I must not love her." For some guys it is easier to stomach the explanation of "falling out of love" or "I must not have truly loved her anyway" than it is to acknowledge their own mean, evil, destructive sin. It is incredibly difficult for so many men to accept and own the reality that the people we love the most are the people we've hurt the worst.[8]

The issue is not about a lack of love. Instead, it's about the depth of love and what loving someone actually means. People who act out sexually often have an understanding of love that is shallow and incomplete. It is typically self-centric with a transactional operating principle behind it. By *transactional*, I mean love is something you give with the expectation you will get something in return. Love is often understood to the extent that it was taught, caught, or experienced in childhood. Think back to our previous conversation on shame and how love was tainted by neglect, abuse, or abandonment. For some, it was simply nonexistent. Still others learned that love was a function of behavior instead of being—as long as they did the right things or stayed out of trouble, then there was love and acceptance. They never knew what it was like to be loved in spite of their behavior; there were always conditions. They've never experienced being loved simply for the sake of being themselves.

The ironic paradox in this is that someone who struggles with sexual integrity issues knows intuitively that love is unconditional and predicated on being. That is partly what the sexual acting out offers. For a brief moment, there are no requirements, and the risk of rejection is low. Through sexualization, they can feel loved and accepted, and the weight of responsibility and feelings of failure are removed, despite everything else wrong in their lives. Even though they are doing wrong in that very moment, there is a calm in the chaos.

How Do We Even Talk about This?

For someone in a relationship with a sexual struggler, especially a spouse, the tendency to heap on shame is real and appealing. Because the pain of sexual betrayal is so personal, many spouses react with statements, accusations, and expressions that actually tap into the core wounds of the addict. Here are a few I frequently hear:

- You're a monster.
- You're a pervert.
- You don't deserve love.
- You're stupid.
- You deserve to be alone.
- You ought to be ashamed of yourself.
- You call yourself a Christian?
- You're a sad excuse for a husband.

Saying these things is completely understandable but not helpful or recommended. The person struggling's unfortunate response to these statements will likely be exactly the opposite of what the hurt spouse desires. Instead of giving her compassion and empathy, the addict will hit her with more defensiveness and contempt. The spouse was hoping that the person who struggles with sexual integrity issues would lean into ownership and humility, but instead, he displays arrogance and shifts the blame to her. This is because when that core wound gets tapped, it actualizes the threefold message of shame—"I am worthless, unlovable, and unforgivable"—and makes self-preservation paramount.

Theoretically, what happens is the core wounds connect to the heart of the kid. The points of origin for the wounds are sometimes specific moments and other times thematic periods of life. Examples include a particular instance of sexual abuse by a pastor or the year of turmoil where one's parents divorced. It may be as broad-sweeping as the whole of junior high. Whether covert or overt, for some people, those injuries stunt further healthy emotional development. The abuse creates a template in their brains that defines how the experience feels, who it involves, and what outcome is to be expected. For the addict in adulthood, in the midst of a tumultuous, angry, painful interaction with his wife whom he has hurt, the template gets activated. The kid is feeling the overwhelming emotion within the man's body, and the adult has a voice to react that the child typically didn't. It all sounds sort of psycho-babbly, but in those moments, the angry wife is dealing with a scared little boy inside of her husband.

To that end, I consistently have wives in my office say they feel like they are dealing with a child when they have those tense moments with their husbands. A few years ago, I had a couple in my office who were in the pit of new disclosure. She was reeling from the news of his infidelity and launched into an expletive-filled expression of her pain. His face began to turn red, and he hardly looked up from the floor. He sank into the leather chair, his fingers interwoven and his hands squeezed between his knees. You could see his anger boiling, and at the same time, he was soaking in shame. The wife moved from expressing the hurt of what he'd done into direct shaming, calling him a worthless pervert and a "sorry excuse for a human." He looked up and glared at her, saying something defensive and finishing with, "I know you are, but what am I?"

Seriously? I thought. *Did he just say that? That was straight out of elementary school!*

It stopped both his wife and me in our tracks, but for different reasons. I asked if she realized what the heck had just happened. She nodded and yelled, saying it's the same thing that happens every time they get into it. He makes some juvenile comment to shut down the conversation and then leaves. When I asked him if he realized what just happened, he had no clue. He also explained how it always goes and how, if she would be less ugly and hostile, he wouldn't say hurtful things and leave. Neither of them could see the juvenile comment was just that: the boy in the man's body.

Think about what would happen if a nine-year-old jumped into the driver's seat of a running bulldozer in the middle of the city. With that kid pulling levers, hitting buttons, and cranking the steering wheel around while punching the gas, the result is going to be chaos and destruction. In effect, that's what happens when shame is tapped and the kid gets activated.

I mentioned previously that a template was created in childhood that informs the stressful situation. Part of that template includes the people involved. With that in mind, in the heat of conflict when shame gets tapped, the person often begins reacting to the person in the template, not the one standing in front of them. Let's say the template includes an angry father who would belittle the child. When the child would try to explain why he made a mistake or did something wrong, the father would yell and demand silence. That child learned to have no voice, and so the template is that when you are getting belittled and accused, you shrink into shame. But in the man's body—the bulldozer, so to speak—the child has a voice and power. He might say things like "You won't cut me down," "I won't let you walk all over me," "You don't have a right to punish me," or something similar. Ultimately, he is responding to the angry father, not the hurt spouse, using a voice he never had.

For the spouse, it is incredibly confusing. It starts to create self-doubt. She starts to wonder if she is losing her mind, if she's overreacting, or if in fact she is the one doing something wrong. Her anger is a righteous anger; it is a right response to injustice. But the feedback says it is mean, demeaning, and sinful. This internal dialogue creates anxiety: perhaps she is making matters worse or maybe even somehow caused the person struggling to do this. It is crazy making!

The Whole Story

When we sign up for a life with someone, the Bible makes clear that we are no longer only two distinct entities. As we seal the covenant of marriage before God, two begin the process of becoming one. We know from Mark 10:8 that "the two become one flesh" in marriage. In a miraculous and mysterious way, when this happens, it becomes a scenario in which the whole is greater than the sum of its parts. The two who are becoming one don't lose themselves; instead, they become more fully themselves and simultaneously more fully integrated. Mysterious indeed.

I believe there is an often-overlooked point to this unique relational combination, though. The focus is consistently present and forward-looking. Our perspective of the union originates at the point of vow taking. When we're in front of meaningful friends and family, and we say "I do" or "I will," we see it as the first official integration. However, this is too narrow a view. Our perspective here is too limited. We fail to account for the past.

We don't frequently talk about the totality of our lives with respect to the union of marriage. The day Shelley and I got married was the day, officially, that all of my past became her present and future—and vice versa. We don't start our stories upon the pastor's blessing; we drag baggage right up to the altar with us! When you marry someone, you are marrying into that person's entire life—from birth to this very moment. Sure, we get to write the script going forward together, but that doesn't erase the script that was written while we were apart. When entering into the relational restoration process, I can't help but begin with this view in mind.

And the point of the full story is to benefit both the person struggling and the spouse.

To begin the healing process, I am a fan of having the struggler write his entire sexual history out. I want to know everything from his earliest memories of playing doctor with a cousin to experimenting in junior high to seeing porn on Dad's Commodore 64. I want to know his relationship history from high school dating all the way up to today. I want to know if there was sexual abuse and, if so, when, how often, by whom, and who knew about it. I suggest that he quantify it all if possible. How many times did he visit strip clubs? How much money did he spend on a mistress? How many hours did he look at porn? How many sexual encounters did he have before the marriage?

The point here isn't to belabor the shame and make him feel worse about himself. It is to begin to understand the gravity of the story as well as the themes. Remember, we don't land at a point in life where we've blown everything up by making one bad decision. It has been a prolonged period of poor choices and micro decisions that have led to this macro outcome. Sexual betrayal is not the byproduct of someone being a monster or pervert, as we discussed. There's a reason he landed here. Writing out the story begins to paint this picture.

Further, it helps the struggler integrate the story. I can't tell you how many men I talk to who say they cannot believe this is their story. Looking in the rearview mirror at all the carnage is shocking. Writing the story begins to help them make sense of how they got to this point as well as the gravity of the impact it has on their loved ones. I recommend husbands read the story aloud to their wives. Hearing themselves reading it can also help solidify it and integrate it.

For the spouse, I recommend you first listen to your husband read it, then hang on to it. Some wives don't want to do either. They do not want to know the story of the past, especially when prior marriages are involved. I respect that as the wife's prerogative. You have to decide for yourself what you need to know. Hearing and reading the story can be sickening. However, for many wives, there is relief. It can feel comforting in a weird way to know the whole story. Much like for the struggler, it can help make sense of how things got to this point.

I've had many wives hear the premarriage story and almost instantly develop a new empathy for their husbands. In one particular case, the wife knew nothing of the sordid sexual experiences her husband had endured before he was twelve. Once she heard the story, she realized that he hardly stood a chance of having a healthy sexuality. It was warped by the influences of childhood in such a way that holding sex, virginity, intimacy, and selfless love in high regard was like fiction to him. The empathy that came from the story did not stop her pain. It did not diminish or excuse how badly he had hurt her. It simply gave her another glimpse of the greater reality that her husband wasn't a monster. It also softened her heart a tick, preparing her for the forgiveness work ahead.

Another reason the written sexual story helps is that it gives the person struggling's wife a narrative for her own story. Remember all that invisible baggage at the altar? No matter how good the premarital counseling, you just can't get at all that plays into life.

Some things only become visible once there is challenge. It's that whole "burning off the dross" thing. The intensity of marital situations and life bring out the impurities of character. The written story then can help a wife through the grieving process because it helps her make sense of her story. She can begin to turn over those puzzle pieces we talked about. In a way, by having the full story, some of the work of turning the pieces faceup is already done for her. Now she has to sort them out and begin putting together the edges and corners.

A Million Questions

As we discussed in the grieving section, it is important to ask questions. You have to in order to make sense of what has happened. Yet inevitably, husband and wife alike wonder how much detail is too much, and they wonder how long a questioning period should last. Is there a statute of limitations on asking? These questions are some of the most difficult to answer with a blanket statement. Because every situation is unique and every situation has an intrinsic dynamic that is the culmination of that couple's story, there is again no formula. Let me share with you how this went at our house.

When Shelley first suspected an affair, she confronted me, and I lied about it. I also shut the door on further questions. I told her the past was the past and that, as a godly woman, she should forgive me and move on. It would also be disrespectful to bring it up again. My comments were twisted and manipulative. Anyway, fast-forward nine months, and she had talked to the mistress and gotten details about the affair. When she confronted me this time, she wasn't willing to let up until she got the full story. There was so much secrecy, so many vagaries the first time that she was committed to it being completely different this go-round. In fact, today, she would tell you she knows more than she wished she knew. Some details cannot be deleted from the hard drive of your mind. So how much is too much? Here are a few things to think about as you engage in asking questions.

Limited Comparisons

When you begin asking questions that have obvious opportunities for comparison, you are moving into murky water. Hair color and style, bra size or other physical features, words spoken, clothing worn or not worn, and physical or sexual acts all fall into this category. When most wives have this information in their heads, they almost cannot help but compare themselves. This infiltrates day-to-day life. It becomes difficult to go to Target, the kids' ball games, school drop-off, and simple social or work functions without the anxiety of comparison. Further, once wives have this comparable information in their heads, it can become an anxiety double-whammy. They walk through life struggling with comparing themselves to other women while simultaneously having to worry about their husband doing the same thing. It can be anxiety overload, and I've known several wives describe the experience legitimately as a panic attack.

Further, these comparison data points make future sexual intimacy more challenging than it otherwise might be. You do not want that junk on your mind and causing strife down the road when things are better and there has been some redemption. This comparison category all seems most applicable to an affair, but it also applies to details of what was viewed in pornography.

There are a couple of caveats here. First, you need to know if there has been any child pornography. If this is the case, the line of legality has been crossed, as has a line signaling the depth of the struggle. Viewing child pornography requires serious counseling and community support. If it hasn't already been reported, it is incumbent upon you to tell the authorities. This is outrageously painful, and I am so, so sorry if you find yourself facing that phone call. Yet you must. For his sake. For their sakes. Further, you need to take steps to protect your kids if they are younger and cannot protect themselves. Even though it may seem impossible, you simply cannot take a chance here.

Second, you should know if there has been anything violent in the pornography. This includes bondage, dominance, sadism, or masochism (BDSM). No, this is not normal, fun, adventurous, sexy, exciting, spicy, or exotic. Never mind what the current landscape of books and movies tell you. This is nonsense, degrading the very experience of dignity and original intimate design and divorcing it from its spiritual meaning. To stand against this warped and dysfunctional idea of sexual experience is neither prudish nor legalistic; it is righteously honoring God's original design. Further, when this is present in the pornographic material or in the physical acting out, it usually points to a deeper heart issue. It often gives expression and manifestation to internal shame in the form of humiliation and power/control differentials. By recognizing this, the counseling and help you receive can focus special attention here.

A final word on this area of comparison: Do not try to compete. Whatever you do, do not succumb to the temptation to match up to or compete with any of these comparison items. It is sad to see a wife lose herself to live up to the unrealistic expectations of her husband. From Botox and breast implants to trying "kinky" stuff in the bedroom, and from driving different cars to heli-skiing, I've seen wives try to change themselves and their lifestyles to live up to the comparison. It's not worth it, and it won't change anything. The issue isn't you. It's not your fault. And nothing you could do or say would fix it. Please, stay you.

Shelley's Thoughts

If comparison was an Olympic event, I'd have a gold medal. I had no idea how destructive comparison could be until we were dealing with marital fallout. As Jason mentioned in the first chapter, I tried to change who I was in order to save our marriage when I knew something was awry but didn't know the extent of Jason's acting out. I willingly told him we could move on from the past, and in so doing, I decided to be the one to fix our problems. I booked trips, I changed my style of clothing, I tried to become a sexy wife. I was determined to be sexy in the bedroom although I walked away feeling empty and used, like I was a prostitute.

The worst thing I could do was take responsibility for Jason's actions and, in so doing, try to change myself from the outside in order to fix our marriage. The only thing this did for me was send me further into despair, hardening my heart even more.

Don't for a second think that if you were younger, if you didn't have stretch marks, if you could shed those last fifteen pounds—whatever it might be—then everything would be fine. And don't think that changing who you are will fix your husband. It won't. As Jason said, you should just be you.

Risky Business

Another subset of details you do need to know are those that put you at physical, financial, or relational risk. Physically, you need to know if there has been any form of physical contact where disease transmission could occur. This includes unprotected sexual acts, kissing, or sharing food, drinks, or utensils. If any of these have occurred, you need to see your doctor and get tested. Do not delay, as embarrassing and disgraceful as it is.

Regarding financial risk, you need to know how, how much, and where money was spent on this. Was it spent on porn, strippers, or a mistress's electric bills? You also need to know where that money came from. Are we talking skimming from paychecks, taking a little extra out of the ATM, or raiding the savings and 401(k)s? Moreover, has there been any fraud committed? Was this funded through the business or a work expense account? And finally, depending on your situation, is there any chance of extortion? Unfortunately, I've seen all these scenarios happen in reality. You have every right to know the truth of your financial risk in this situation.

As it pertains to relational risk, you need to know if people close to you were involved. This includes friends, neighbors, babysitters, family members, and other people in your community. There's a special kind of pain, humiliation, and embarrassment a wife feels when she has been unknowingly interacting with an accomplice to her husband's infidelity. Does that make sense? You have a right to know who in your world is that untrustworthy and disrespectful.

There is one nuance here that I would urge you to consider. I want to encourage you to draw a line between what went on in the mind versus what went on in real life. Here again, as a wife, I believe you have every right to know these details, but you have to consider the implications of knowing them. This becomes an issue most poignantly when a man has fantasized about someone in his wife's family. For a wife to find out her husband has lusted after her sister makes every holiday from here on out incredibly difficult and awkward. A man who is working toward recovery, denying himself permission to entertain those thoughts going forward, and praying for God to erase those fantasies may never struggle with those thoughts about that person again. Thus, for you as a wife, knowing that piece of information may create additional pain that is unwarranted going forward. Please don't misunderstand me: I'm not downgrading the pain or minimizing the sin and offense. I do, however, want you to think about the bigger picture in this recovery process. Do you really need to know what went on in his mind if he never acted on it? Only you can decide.

Time Is *Not* Running Out

While working through all this with our counselor, he insisted (read: beat into me) that there were no restrictions and no timeline or statute of limitations on Shelley asking questions. It was hard for me to get my mind around this. I kept thinking, "Great, my counselor is giving my wife a free pass to beat me over the head with my sin for the rest of my life." In reality, my counselor wasn't setting me up for a life of pain. He was setting us up for healing. I was a selfish man who couldn't see beyond the immediacy of my own pain, and I didn't have the ability at the moment to grasp the bigger picture. I was also blind to the fact that my counselor saw I lacked the resiliency to hold my wife's pain, and this prescription was intended to help me develop it.

In the beginning, the intense, rapid-fire interrogation was regular. We're talking night after night, hours on end. Then we would be back at it again when Shelley woke up at three a.m. with it all on her mind. Like most wives I talk to today, Shelley would get so spun up in the anger and pain, she would ask questions she really didn't want the answer to. I could ask her if she were sure she wanted me to respond, but invariably, she would demand the answer. Again, she felt she had been duped the first time around, and she wasn't going to let it happen again. So many of her questions were rhetorical questions too: "Why?," "What were you thinking?," "How could you?" No answer could suffice. We also circled the same barn over and over again. Shelley would ask the same questions repeatedly, sometimes verbatim. Just because an answer had seemed satisfactory and the issue settled on Monday night didn't mean it wasn't fair game on Tuesday morning. This all went on for the better part of the first nine months.

Going into the second year of our recovery, the questions diminished dramatically. Shelley had come to some resolution, had resigned that some things would never make sense, and also realized her quest for knowledge wasn't helping. However, there were still questions; they weren't off-limits. And there still are some. We still need to have those conversations about the past, but they are different today. This is due in part to how I have a different perspective now and understand that the questions are rooted in fear.

Love Fights Fear

It is important to recognize that fear is the primary emotion that drives this questioning. Fear breeds the out-of-control feelings and anxiety that lead to wives feeling that sense of free fall. Asking questions, getting answers, and being in what feels like a position of power takes the edge off. It falsely gives one a sense of being in control and managing further pain. It takes away the unknowns and instills at least a semblance of stability. Today I recognize that any time Shelley has a question about the past, it is rooted in fear. She may not even recognize this; it may seem innocuous and simply like a data point. But somewhere deep down, it has its root in wondering what the future holds.

I find it interesting that Scripture teaches us that fear is mitigated by love. 1 John 4:18 tells us, "There is no fear in love." You've probably heard it said that perfect love casts out fear.

In other words, to love my wife well is to create an environment that is safe and secure, mitigating anything that might jeopardize her heart. Answering her questions humbly and honestly honors her request to feel safe. After causing so much damage and creating a frightening environment for her, the least I can do is try to calm those fears by answering her questions.

With this idea in mind, we can reframe the question regarding the statute of limitations. Rather than asking how long is permissible to bring up the painful questions, we should instead ask when is it no longer okay to try to mitigate the fear. Granted, you can certainly beat your husband up over the questions you have and his answers to them. But if your motivation for the questions is to yet again find reassurance and security, you won't do that. You'll simply be inviting your husband into a business that he is already called to work in: the fear mitigation business. At our house, there is no expiration date on Shelley asking questions. I'm never getting fired from my career as a fear mitigator. And I don't want to be.

Paradox for Wives

Being in a relationship with someone struggling with sexual integrity issues creates a dichotomy or paradox. Tension can develop regarding who or what is in need of healing. The struggler needs healing, the spouse needs healing, and then there's the relationship. It can even begin to feel like a competition. Many wives I talk to say it starts to create bitterness or resentment too. Wives want to figure out how to make it through the damaging effects of sexual sin but intrinsically know they are bound in some way by their husbands' willingness to change. The wife wants to find stable ground, yet she is chained to the roller coaster ride that is her spouse.

So whose healing comes first? And what is a wife to do while the process is unfolding and getting worked out? Should she separate and draw hard boundary lines? Love her husband unconditionally and without pushback? When is it time to deal with marital issues that preceded all the sexual integrity issues? These questions all seem to loom large for the wives I interact with. The whole thing can feel like one giant question mark. My hope for this section is to answer some of these questions.

Old Frameworks

I think it is important to frame this with traditional thoughts on healing from sexual betrayal. There have largely been two schools of thought on dealing with these issues. The first defines betrayal as a marital issue and thus implies it is a function of marital problems. The second swings the pendulum the other way and puts a harsh spotlight on the individual work. Let's look at the marital perspective first.

Sexual Addiction as a General Marital Issue

The basis for this perspective is that something in the marriage caused the sexual integrity issues. Aspects of the relationship could have been adjusted, and that might have prevented the betrayal. Or, turning toward healing, changing enough relationally will function as an insurance policy to protect against future violations. Typically, when I see someone in my office who has been exposed to this perspective, they report suggestions regarding date nights, love languages, parenting arrangements, sexual frequency, physical desirability—as in "Wife, you need to lose some weight and get dolled up more often." No, I'm not kidding.

Going a bit further, I have talked to many couples for whom the pivotal point of this perspective rested on differing values and preferences around sexual intimacy. Specifically, the sexual integrity issues weren't viewed as damaging or dysfunctional. Instead, they were assessed to be values and thus should not be vilified. Where the husband and wife differed on these "values," accommodation or adoption was expected. In other words, if the husband is using porn, then the wife should adopt it as a part of their sexual intimacy. If that is not acceptable to her, then she is the one with the problem; she is too naive, prudish, or straight-laced and should accommodate his viewing. Likewise, if one spouse desires sexual variety in the form of other partners, then the other spouse should adopt and join in the swinging parties or accommodate and find a way to be okay with promiscuity. To be clear, this advice has come from Christian counselors! I'm not sure what Bible they are reading, but it's not the one about a God who holds sexual, marital intimacy in high regard as a reflection of Himself.

I nearly despise this perspective—I'll admit that right out of the gate. There may be a myriad of marital problems that create a dysfunctional, unhappy, and bitter environment to live in. The marriage might have been sexless for decades. There may even be prior infidelity. But marital dissatisfaction and betrayal of one spouse do not cause betrayal or sexual integrity issues on the part of the other. There are so many other options to deal with the discord and pain. No amount of future "marital satisfaction" precludes sexual betrayal. The tragedy of this perspective, in my opinion, is that it overlooks the issues going on within the heart of the betrayer. It addresses symptoms, not their root causes.

Sexual Addiction as an Individual Issue

The second approach, and probably the more prolific one, is a highly individualistic view of the issue. It sits at the other end of the spectrum, parsing the marriage and delineating between his issues, her issues, and the marital entity. The core premise is that the person with sexual integrity issues has to do his own personal healing while the marriage is sort of on "pause." While it doesn't blame the marriage for the sexual betrayal, it does place the marriage in a subordinate position. The underlying assumption is that once the individuals do work to get healthy, they will then land in a healthy marriage. It implies equal contributions to the postbetrayal relationship.

Further, a consistent assumption in this perspective is that the person married to the addict is probably codependent, enmeshed, and enabling. Thus the spouse has to do his or her own healing work at the same time as the betrayer. Again, all the while, the marriage is hanging in the balance. Some therapists who take this approach will even draw rigid lines between what is his and her recovery work to the point that a wife isn't allowed to ask what her husband is doing in counseling sessions, groups, and so on. To do so would qualify as codependent. A phrase that is endemic to this perspective is "Each person is responsible for his own side of the street." In other words, don't be involved in the other person's healing work.

While it is true that there may be elements of enmeshment and codependency in a relationship where someone struggles with sexual addiction, this individualistic approach negates the reality of self-protection on the wife's behalf. What's more, many wives want to know what is going on in their husbands' sessions not just because of their fear or codependency but to give them hope! Knowing what kind of good, solid recovery work their husbands are doing encourages wives. To bifurcate the process into his healing and her healing takes away an opportunity for hope, and sometimes that is the only thing a wife is clinging to.

Speaking of losing hope, when the marriage is left in the balance, waiting for two unhealthy people to get healthy, it can feel pretty dark. The question of "whether we'll make it" is constantly on the horizon. Granted, that's true regardless of the perspective taken to fix things, but with the individualistic approach, marital restoration is almost viewed as something to be addressed in the future. In my experience, both for Shelley and me as well as in my office with folks in the middle of the destruction, that's simply unrealistic. The marriage is affected in the moment, and how to do relationship on a random Tuesday evening is a big question. It can't just wait. It has to be addressed in conjunction with the other work that is happening.

Finally, in this individualistic approach, a third counselor is often recommended, one specific to the marriage. So now we have his, hers, and theirs. Sometimes this is required by state rules and regulations for mental health practitioners, and sometimes it is simply a philosophy adhered to by the counselors. Can you imagine the disjointed care and advice given to couples in the process when these approaches are mixed together? But I'm not getting on another soapbox for now. Rather, I'd like to suggest a new perspective.

A New Perspective

Sexual Addiction as an Integrated Issue

To begin, let's view the process as an integrated whole of three entities—him, her, and the marriage. At any given time, what he is doing is affecting her and impacting the marriage. Likewise, the same holds true for the wife. How she operates affects both her husband and the marriage. There is constant interplay between them. With the previous approaches we discussed, one of them gets downplayed, minimized, or overlooked. The general marital approach negates the unique dynamic of the individual, while the individualistic approach hyperfocuses and overlooks the marital dynamic. When restoration and redemption are in mind, we must address each entity and the interplay between them. Remember that I'm not insinuating in any way causation. Neither the wife nor the marriage *causes* a husband's sexual integrity issues. Instead, what I'm insisting is that healing from these issues holistically is possible. Sure, sometimes there are issues so deep, so psychologically disordered, and the relationship is so damaged that it necessitates individual work before the marriage can be reengaged. I think that is far more often the exception than the rule though. With that in mind, here's the perspective Shelley and I recommend.

The focus of counseling runs two paths. One is working on understanding his struggle, background, why he acts out, how to help him not act out again, and what long-term recovery and sanctification looks like. We're working on his junk. The other path is focused on marital restoration. We're working on providing security to the wife, rebuilding trust, helping offset fear and triggers, and creating a new relational dynamic. While doing this work, I want the wife to be present in the sessions the whole time.

There are three reasons for this, born out of the three distinct roles a wife plays. The first is listener/learner. It can be beneficial for a wife to listen to what is being taught and to begin to understand what the sexual integrity issues are really about. It can also be helpful for a wife to hear her husband interact with the counselor and share in the discoveries and insights that are made.

Further, wives can confirm or deny the information being shared by the man in the hot seat. This is the second role: consultant. I consider a wife to be 50 percent of my window into her husband's world. As a wife, she can tell me things about him that he can't or won't. She can give insight into his story that he is blind to. Sure, a wife's perceptions are her reality and can be skewed; there is a risk that her reality is inaccurate. But as a counselor, even that input is helpful because that new perspective on restoration, the clash of realities, gives a window into the marital entity. Two disparate and distinct perspectives on the relationship can provide an informative look into the dynamic that was formed before and during the betrayal. Reshaping both his and her realities and forming a new narrative of the marriage is part of recovery.

And that leads to the third role: wife. As we work through the process, there are points when wives need to know what to do next. They need guidance on how to express anger, how to ask questions, when to trust or when not to, how to talk about the issues, what to do about sex, and so on. These questions inevitably arise, and answering them in the context of the couple just makes sense. It gives her the answers she needs, it gives him perspective and a sense of what the ground rules are (which are always lopsided and weighted in her favor), and then, as a couple, they know the operating parameters.

I try to tell everyone that walks into my office that my perspective on recovery, and frankly on marriage as a whole, is that we as husbands bear 90 percent of the burden of restoration while wives bear 10 percent. And usually, addressing her 10 percent is down the road, not immediate. I approach it this way because of Ephesians 5:25–28. Nowhere in the Bible, per my understanding, is there a verse that puts marriage as a fifty-fifty deal. No verses indicate a wife's responsibility is to die on her husband's behalf.

One thing I do want to address here is the request for individual counseling for the husband. Fairly often, I'll have men ask if we can do individual counseling and sort of alternate between that and marital work. Rarely do I agree to this, and the reason is that, in my opinion, most of what we'll deal with individually can benefit the marriage as a whole. Anything that needs to be discussed without the wife present, outside of her own request to be absent, is potentially lost relational mileage. And the reality is, more often than not, when a husband requests individual time, it's usually just to vent about all the work his wife isn't doing, the problems she has, and so on. Sometimes a session or two of this without a wife present can be beneficial. It sort of clears the deck for the husband, and he feels heard and understood. The place where I do consistently make the exception to alternate individual and marital work is when the wife insists on it. If she wants to opt out of some of the sessions and give him a chance to vent or ask questions that she doesn't want the answers to, then I'll usually acquiesce. The primary driver, though, is empowerment and care for her. A wife needs to have a voice after betrayal stifles and takes her voice away.

All this being said, with this 90/10 perspective, we have to acknowledge that within a wife's 10 percent, there is much work to be done. The question becomes, When is it time for her work to begin? This leads to another aspect of this new perspective: typically, rather than insisting that a wife jump into her own counseling, Shelley and I prefer to have a wife engage a healing community. Finding a support group with like-minded women and a leader who understands the process of healing is imperative. In Shelley's groups, the facilitators have all been through betrayal and marital restoration. Support groups can be dicey because they can easily become husband-bashing sessions. Of course, there are always moments of venting and anger, but that is different than a consistent negative theme. There should be careful oversight to ensure that, while the group processes the pain of the past, they don't lose sight of the redemption that is possible in the present and future. Working through a helpful curriculum—such as the one in Shelley's book, *Rescued: A Woman's Guide to Surviving and Thriving after Sexual Betrayal*—can guide the group and keep it from devolving into a negative space. Some wives do find they need more intensive help than a support group can provide, and individual counseling can be the right fit for them. Again, we want that counseling to have marital restoration in mind as the individual work happens. I've heard too many horror stories of wives going to counselors who espouse a mantra of "You should be happy, and that may require you to be apart from him" rather than "Let's figure out how to find a healthy you in the context of this relationship and exhaust all options before we start looking at what it would mean to be out of this relationship." The difference is hopefully obvious.

This perspective of dealing with sexual integrity as an integrated issue targets hope and restoration. It requires patience and humility as virtues and also provides a constant reminder of our need for Jesus. If there is to be redemption, it will be by the Lord's grace.

Shelley's Thoughts

I'm going to tell you this straight up: if Jason or our counselor had insisted on us working through this from a marital perspective, where I was told to work on date nights and sexual intimacy, or from an individualistic perspective, where I was told to stay on my side of the street and focus on myself, it would have most certainly been the demise of our marriage. All I could manage was to step back from Jason and watch him while working toward trusting our counselor. Quickly thereafter, I needed to work toward feeling however I felt and owning those feelings, which meant expressing those feelings to Jason (using my voice) and connecting in a place where I felt safe and supported (this came in the context of relationships with strong, wise women who were working through betrayal themselves).

I can't even begin to tell you how healing it was for me to simply (although not easily) focus on how I felt, use my voice, and keep my deserved front-row seat to watch Jason's process.

Measuring Progress

"How do I know if he's healing or changing?" "How do I know if I can trust him?" "When will he be different?" All these questions have the same root in common—namely, trying to determine how to measure progress. Most wives want to feel safe enough to go back in the water, but they are scared to even dip a toe in. The signs that it is worth trying or risking are vague and variable. There are no clear markers. To further complicate things, in the early stages, we are measuring against the past. The metric that we naturally default to is how broken things were before, measuring against the past: "Is my husband doing what he used to do, saying what he used to say, being the way he used to be—or not?" Therefore, to calculate the risk of reengaging, the algebra requires some variable of "badness" or "sinfulness." If he's not as bad as he used to be or as sinful as he used to be, then it is safe—or so goes the logic. I'm terrible at math, so this whole analogy breaks down for me! Thus finding a better way to measure progress is important. There are two factors I like to take into account in doing so.

Quantitative versus Qualitative Recovery Work

As a wife looking toward healing and hoping for change, you want to see your husband take all the steps necessary. As he does so, there is a frenzy of activity that, over time, can feel like it follows the law of diminishing returns. He's doing a bunch of recovery stuff, but things don't seem to be getting better. The reason for this is often because there is a difference between quantitative and qualitative recovery work.

Quantitative recovery work refers to the logistics and the specific tasks associated with recovery. These are the counseling appointments and group meetings, being diligent about making it to church and Bible study, the books he is reading and the homework he is doing. It can also refer to the new boundaries and lifestyle changes he has put in place, such as doing away with one-on-one meetings with women, decreasing his work travel, not watching movies or TV, replacing his smartphone with a "dumb" phone, and so on. All of these tactical moves are important; don't think I'm downplaying that. The logistics of recovery are real. You have to change your lifestyle in order to change on the whole. The problem comes when all you're doing is changing your behavior and the logistics are not translating into heart work. This is what the qualitative aspect is all about.

Qualitative recovery work asks, "What difference does it all make?" Yes, there are all these logistical changes, but are they making a difference in the way he thinks, acts, feels, talks, and walks? Quantitative work deals with the tasks of recovery, while qualitative work is the texture of recovery. It is deeper and character-oriented. When a man is actually working his recovery and allowing God to change his heart, he is consistently asking himself what difference it all makes. He's not simply going through the motions. If he is, the logistics will quickly become recovery hoop-jumping. This is a painful place for a wife. It can start to feel desperate. In my office, a wife will ask me what else her husband can do because it feels like they are stalling. When I ask him what else he's doing, he'll rattle off a huge list of all the tactical things he is doing, followed by a statement about how he's doing everything he can but nothing is ever good enough, or something similar. This is a clue that the qualitative work is lacking. In order to get the most out of the recovery work and move from task to texture, I like to ask these three questions weekly:

1. What am I learning about *God*?
2. What am I learning about *myself*?
3. What am I learning about *others*?

In my own journey, even today, if I can answer these questions with confidence, I know I'm becoming a different man. But the reality is, I have to mine the recovery work to get the nuggets that answer these questions. For example, when I'm reading a book that is recovery-oriented, I have to be asking myself how it connects to my story, what it could change, and how I'll apply it. When I talk to men I'm accountable to, I have to be attuned to what they are saying and how they are saying it and also in touch with my humility to receive their feedback. Then, taking their input, I must engage my heart and look for a way I can live life differently. When I'm in the Word, I like to put myself in the story and see through the protagonists' eyes, asking what God might want to teach me about Himself or myself or someone else. I'm trying hard not to "check the box" of doing the discipline of reading the Bible (though sometimes it definitely is just that). My point with this is not to set the expectation that you must have a revelation or profound insight every day. It doesn't work that way—at least, not in my life. Instead, the qualitative aspect of recovery is about developing a consistent lifestyle of reflection and a willingness to see what God might be up to in me and the world around me. The quantitative aspects of recovery are simply the positions and circumstances I intentionally put myself in to facilitate that lifestyle.

If you find yourself wondering if there is forward progress or if the recovery process is stalling, it may behoove you to have a conversation with your spouse about these two distinct aspects of recovery. It may be that you want to implement a regular check-in conversation where these three questions are asked and answered. Shelley and I were putting together a video on this recently, and she pop-quizzed me, asking me to answer the questions on the spot. I didn't know what she was going to ask, and it caught me a bit off guard. You can check out the video here: http://redemptiveliving.com/measuring-progress/.

CHAPTER SEVEN

What If It's Not Working?

Truth be told, I don't even want to write this section of the book. I've been avoiding it. It shouldn't have to be included, yet it's a familiar reality. Some men won't lean into the process of change. I hold out eternal hope that every leopard can change its spots by the work of the Holy Spirit in us. It is by and through Jesus that the impossible becomes possible. But some people simply refuse to change. They have become so deeply entrenched in their comfortable dysfunction that it feels functional. To get healthy would require things to be uncomfortable, disrupting a status quo that is so damaging yet seemingly manageable. So what is a wife to do when this is the case? Divorce can't be the only option. It is not the only option. There are plenty of steps to take between discovery and divorce. Those steps come in the form of boundaries.

Boundaries versus Needs Requests

To begin, it can be helpful to delineate between boundaries and needs requests. It may sound like semantics, but the two have a different texture and tone to them. I like how Shelley explains it in *Rescued*: "A need request is typically something we use to invite our husbands to stop or start doing in order to improve our sense of security. Think of needs requests as being related to triggers. On the other hand, typically a boundary is something we use in order to protect ourselves from further hurt, fear, anxiety, and insecurity."[9]

A need request is an invitation. It is vulnerable. It is actually a confession of permeability, pointing to some area of life that feels risky. It gives a husband an opportunity to practice protecting his wife and reverse the trend of her dealing with fear alone. It's a chance to *love* her, as we discussed in Chapter 6.

A boundary is different from a need request, though they sometimes do overlap. A boundary is a statement of impermeability. It is not so much an invitation as it is a declaration. It's an announcement, not a discussion. Most of the time, needs requests are categorized as "what to do," while boundaries fall into the category of "what *not* to do."

Boundaries

When we talk about boundaries, we have to remember that boundaries are for protection, not punishment. It is easy to think boundaries are about exacting consequences on the person for his poor choices: "If you continue to do this bad or wrong thing, then this is what you'll get." That is not really the point of boundaries, though it is often a by-product. Think of boundaries as protecting instead of punishing. Boundaries are the force fields that keep out harmful and destructive projectiles coming your way. Notice I didn't say that it keeps out "the enemy"; this is intentional. The person who has hurt you through sexual betrayal is not the enemy. Boundaries put you in a position of protection so that when there is pain, the intensity is lessened on some level. In fact, healthy boundaries on your part will help you refrain from vilifying the other person because you'll have a measure of insulation from the most intense pain, thus keeping you from reaching that nuclear place.

When and What

Healthy boundaries come in many forms, but they all aim toward the same goal: minimizing the devastation to your heart. Figuring out when to implement them and what exactly to put in place is challenging. There is no real right or wrong answer to this because the boundaries have to match your situation. Here are some considerations to factor in as you map your path forward.

Defensiveness and Blameshifting

A husband's defensiveness is typically a sign of either guilt or shame. When there is something to defend, there is usually something to hide. Per our previous discussion, when a person violates his conscience by acting out or doing something that goes against his core values, he ends up draining his compassion tank, and empathy wanes. When a husband is defensive or blameshifting (making his wife the problem rather than taking ownership), it can sometimes be a sign of an empty compassion tank.

However, sometimes it is no longer borne out of hiding and guilt but comes from shame instead. When that threefold message of shame gets tapped, we want the shame to stop, and we'll lash out, trying to get it off of us. Yet the explanation for this behavior does not excuse it. For a wife seeking reconciliation, the pain of betrayal is enough. She feels like he is adding insult to injury when he then discounts or turns the tables on her. And she should not accept this behavior. It is completely understandable to implement boundaries here. Here are some that I see wives enact:

- They will not have conversations with their husbands first thing in the morning or right before bed.
- They can walk away from a conversation and refuse to reengage until their husbands apologize or until the next day.
- They can insist that their husbands leave the house, regardless of time of day, so that the husbands can collect their thoughts and remember the present reality.
- They can refuse to talk about anything other than logistics (kids' schedules, finances, grocery lists) until their husbands apologize and/or explain what drove their behavior.

Again, none of these are meant to cause a husband pain or to prove how wrong he is. They are meant to protect a wife's heart. Rather than continue to allow pain to be heaped on top of pain, these boundaries empower a wife to limit the impact of her husband's actions. They also send a message to the husband that the old ways are gone and the new ways of respect and dignity are nonnegotiable.

Unwillingness to Engage the Process

Some husbands refuse to take the reins and lead the healing process. Their resistance to change keeps them stuck in the mud and, simultaneously, leaves their wives trapped in limbo. They drop the ball on scheduling counseling sessions, doing homework, reading recovery material, going to group meetings, and so on. They know change is necessary, but the tyranny of the urgent wins the day, and work and life are busy.

They also usually expect, to some degree, that once the dust settles, their wives will drop the subject and everything will smooth over. If the husband shows a bit of effort, it may be just enough to pacify his wife and make her get off his back. This business of only doing work when his wife is on his case is excruciating for every wife I talk to. It can feel like any sense of security or any hope for the future is her responsibility. As a wife, you should not accept this behavior. This is another scenario where you must protect yourself.

When a husband refuses to engage the process, a dichotomy of possibilities is created. On one side, the risk of relapse and acting out again goes up. How can someone expect to live a different life when he isn't doing anything differently? On the other side is a life of changed behavior but the same old heart. For a wife in a postbetrayal relationship, just "not acting out anymore" doesn't cut it. There needs to be restitution and redemption. To protect herself from further pain (potential realities financially, physically, spiritually, and emotionally) she must draw boundaries. For many wives, this begs the question of whether to separate.

Separation

This is one of those boundaries that I have specific opinions on. It can sometimes be helpful, and it can launch a couple into a new phase of recovery. But sometimes it is just the first step toward divorce, which is not what we want. I'd like to make some distinctions and paint a picture of options pertaining to separating.

In-House Separation

Typically, when separation comes up, the idea is for one person or the other to find another place to live. This doesn't have to be the case. In fact, this can actually be a double whammy for the wife, depending on the family's stage in life. For young families, when the husband moves out, the entire parenting load falls on Mom's shoulders. Now not only does she have to deal with the pain of betrayal, but she is punished by having to be a single parent. The result is increased bitterness and resentment toward the husband, which makes the road to restoration more difficult.

I am a fan instead of in-house separations, where the shared duties are still shared. The two main features of in-house separation deal with living quarters and duties. Where each person sleeps is important because of vulnerability. This can look like different bedrooms; different parts of the house, like upstairs/downstairs; or even different portions of the property. I once had a couple who separated, and the husband spent a short stint in a camper trailer nearby. All these locations create enough of a gap in proximity to help the wife feel less vulnerable, yet the husband remains close enough to still be helpful in life. The man who stayed in the camper would return to the house every morning to make breakfast and help get the kids ready for school. In the evenings, he would leave after he helped with the bedtime routines. Along with remaining helpful, in-house (or close-proximity) separation also can make the impact on the kids a bit softer and less disruptive.

If you're not at this stage of life, it might not feel quite as much like a punishment to have your husband living elsewhere. Again, this speaks to the nuance of each couple's situation.

The other reason I like in-house separation is that when the husband truly decides to work and engage, there are more opportunities for the wife to see it. She has more of those small moments where she can catch him operating in real time, off guard and authentically, rather than in a contrived circumstance or scheduled conversation. A man who is inviting God into his moment-to-moment life will definitely make mistakes, and nothing will change overnight, but the moments where things are different will show themselves.

Out-of-House Separation

I am not a fan of out-of-house separations, yet there are times when it is entirely appropriate and necessary. I can't tell you if it is required in your situation or if it will help or hurt, but here are some guidelines.

In situations where physical harm to you or your children is a risk, it is appropriate. In addition, you should research your legal rights and options as well as safeguards like shelter and finances. If he is physically abusive, you should contact the necessary authorities.

When the toxicity of the conversations results in outbursts in front of the kids, it also may be appropriate. By *toxicity*, I mean a couple of things. It may be toxic if they are hearing about details of the acting out or your sexual histories. It may also be toxic if they are seeing unhealthy conflict. I'll provide a note here for both the struggler and the spouse: You must refrain from weaponizing your children. To threaten custody rights, visitation, finances, or the future is going to harm them more than anything. Please, if you find yourself doing this, talk to your support system about it. Ask for accountability and help in this area.

One more scenario where out-of-house separation is justified is when there are persistent lies—lies not just about past behavior but also about present behaviors. I'm talking about more than a gut feeling here. This scenario applies when wives verify lies pertaining to whereabouts, spending, business ventures, hobbies, activities with the kids, and so on. There may be nothing sketchy about the lies in terms of acting out, but operating without integrity in other areas of life can be just as damaging to the relationship and equally disrespectful. Further, lies bring everything into question. When a wife has to endure consistent lying, she eventually starts to feel crazy. She begins to wonder if she'll be alone and left as a single parent or without a nest egg, perhaps spending her later years dealing with the repercussions of his present misconduct. In order to protect her sanity and, on some level, her future, separation can be prudent. In the context of that separation, it usually becomes painfully obvious what his motives and intentions are. What I see is that an unrepentant husband who refuses integration with his wife and is unwilling to live in truth will end up behaving as if he were single. He'll come and go as he pleases, selfishly not considering the impact of his choices on anyone else and relishing the freedom to live in unchecked denial. This exposes the hollowness of his pleas for the wife to reconcile.

Boundaries do frequently have the by-product of being consequences, but that is secondary to their primary function of protection. Figuring out what will serve you on your journey, be it boundaries or needs requests, will help you feel more stable and secure. Many wives don't know what they need in the midst of all the chaos. Some wives do know but feel selfish or disrespectful when asking or implementing ways to ensure that those needs are met. This is another place where a healing community is a critical piece of the recovery process.

Waiting and Watching

I said at the beginning of this chapter that there are steps to take and options available before reaching the point where you should consider divorce. Beyond boundaries and requests for what you need for your safety and security, there is a time where the only thing you can do is wait and watch. It can feel helpless and disempowering, but it truly is not. In fact, it is courageous and requires depth of character.

To wait intentionally is to hold out hope and keep bitterness at bay. It doesn't mean you don't feel; it means you aren't controlled by the emotions. Waiting is more palatable for most wives when there is a time frame. I suggest ninety days as a simple starting point. That's not three months until you decide your entire future, just three months until you decide on the next three months. There need not be a definitive decision date, just points of reassessment.

While waiting, you are practicing watching. This is where character comes in. To wait while the person who has hurt you the most decides whether to allow God to change him is hard. To try to see the best in him while his decisions show you only the worst is painful. It takes Christlike patience. Watching does not mean you relax your boundaries. It's quite the opposite: you keep the

boundaries and requests in place and watch your husband negoti-
ate serving you with respect to them. You aren't trying to make it
easier on him, yet you aren't trying to make it more difficult either.
Watching also means you hold the tension between knowing that
there will be mistakes and that change won't happen overnight
alongside expecting consistent forward momentum. Remember
the idea of quantitative versus qualitative recovery work: you are
looking for the texture among the tasks. As an example of this,
a wife in my office recently recounted a story of a conflict that
began to escalate over the course of a week. On the third or fourth
instance, as the arms race heated up, she braced herself for his usual
spin and blameshifting. She got a tearful smile on her face as she
talked about how he took a deep breath, came to tears himself in
that moment, and simply apologized. It disarmed her, settled them
both, and they had an evening without another check in the "con"
column. That one win wasn't enough for her to say she would
be staying for the long run, but it was enough to wait and watch
another week.

I don't know how long it is prudent for you to wait and watch.
It may be ninety days. It may be six months. If you are in the very
beginning stages of this journey, I would suggest you give it six to
nine months for the dust to begin to settle. It can often take that
long to figure out what is actually salvageable relationally. Your
wait may turn into a year because you are seeing enough consistent change. Remember, it took Shelley nearly eighteen months
of waiting and watching before she decided to recommit to the
marriage. My hope with this short section is to convince you to
practice waiting and watching before you pull the ripcord.

．　．　．

I started this chapter recounting my reluctance to write it. If you find yourself needing the guidance of this chapter, again, I'm sorry. I wouldn't wish this difficulty on anyone. It is bad enough having been betrayed in some way, but for there to be so much uphill in the aftermath is a tremendous injustice. I urge you to remember that you are worth the work of setting and enforcing boundaries. It is an act of dignity to protect your heart, refuse to allow the status quo to continue, and insist on change. All this is contained within the parentheses of grace and waiting, similar to how God interacts with us.

CHAPTER EIGHT

When It's Our Kids

Understanding and loving a sexual addict when he is a spouse is a painful and difficult journey. However, I don't know if there is any situation more challenging and tumultuous than watching our kids struggle with something like this. It is heartbreaking and tragic; it brings up self-doubt, causing us to question our parenting. We wonder where we went wrong, what we did or didn't do to cause it. While a thorough self-assessment may be prudent, we must act decisively to help our kids. The following are a few guidelines for addressing the struggle with them. Bear in mind that for this section, we are focusing on kids still at home.

Content

First, it is important to understand what they are actually struggling with. Much like our conversation earlier regarding the full story, we need to know what our kids have done, had done to them, looked at, or are looking at. I suggest you approach this conversation with gravity while also being mindful not to send a message of shame. Further, we have to remember that our shock can be misinterpreted as shame. If your son or daughter discloses behaviors that you never in your wildest imagination suspected him or her to be involved in, your surprise is valid. I've heard countless stories, though, where the parent's response—in word, tone, and body language—sent a message that was belittling, shame-inducing, and seemed to accuse the child of monstrosity. Remember to allow yourself to feel the heartache beneath the anger, disappointment, and surprise.

Set aside a time to talk about what is happening based on your discoveries (assuming that was the prompt in the first place). Do not play the guessing game with him, waiting to see if he cops to what you already know. I suggest telling him what you already know and asking him to broaden the story from there. Remind him that your goal is to understand, not to exact punishment on him or anyone else.

As you seek to understand, I suggest you move from what your child has done alone to what may have happened with others. Start by understanding what she's been thinking about or has thought of doing. Next, understand what has happened in terms of masturbation, then pornography. Move on from there to what has involved others: conversations in chatrooms, dating/hookups apps, private messages on social media, or with girl- or boyfriends, and physical sexual encounters. You'll have to adjust your questions based on your child's age and maturity. Obviously a ten-year-old cannot express what a seventeen-year-old can. To that end, be careful about leading questions. You can't lead your ten-year-old into admitting something that she doesn't completely understand. For example, "Have you looked at bondage pornography?" is different from "Have you seen pictures or videos of people getting hurt or being mean to each other?"

You also want to ask specifically about sexual contact. Has your child been touched inappropriately? Has he touched someone inappropriately? Is he sexually active, and if so, activity of what types, with whom, and how many times? If he has had consensual sexual activity, was it protected? If the answer is no, you should consider insisting on an STI test.

As painful as it can be to know this information, it is critical to understand what you are dealing with. It may be the early stages of an addiction, and thus intervention will help your child bypass the escalation and further devastation. Or it could be a full-fledged addiction, and intervention could save her life!

Context

Sexual Addiction as a Systemic Issue

You want to understand if this is a function of a larger systemic problem or if it is indeed a problem unto itself. For context, you want to investigate what's happening socially with friends, friends' parents, teachers, pastors, and siblings. Have there been friends who have come in or out of your child's life recently, or has there been a change in who he calls his best friends? Is there a bully who has entered the picture? Has he had trouble assimilating into a new environment after moving to either a new house or school? Perhaps he has recently transitioned into or out of band, sport teams, or debate club or between schools (from middle to high school, or homeschool to public school or vice versa, for example).

You want to factor in other behavioral elements as well. Changes in your child's external expressions of her internal world can be helpful clues. In this sense, you are looking for distinct differences in behavior or appearance. Grades and school reports can be a window into this, but also look for signs of withdrawal from social settings or regular activities, such as church or extracurriculars. The idea is that you want to see if the sexual acting out is acutely addictive in nature or if it is part of a larger story of difficulty and thus more symptomatic. This will guide your steps toward appropriate help.

Sexual Addiction as a Peer-Related Issue

It is also necessary to understand how and when your child is involved in these behaviors. Again, these questions need to be framed as curiosity, not indictment. Is this a situation where friends, teammates, or classmates are involved and thus has a peer-pressure element? One common story I hear is of pornographic pictures of someone (anonymous or not) that are circulated via text. Another involves games played at a party or church event. Remember spin the bottle? The kissing we deemed risky back when we were kids has, in present generations, escalated into sexual acts. Looking at the context, is your child's behavior something that happens in isolation or in social/peer situations?

If the behavior doesn't seem peer related and happens more often in isolation, then you need to understand frequency and location. This can sometimes be a clue to what the acting-out behavior is about. If it happens in the bathroom at school in the middle of the day, it might point to anxiety that is heightened while there. Alternatively, if it happens in bed late at night, it may point to something emotional happening at home. Understanding how often it happens also gives some context to the problem. The frequency of your child's acting out is directly proportional to the level of his underlying pain. Thus if the acting out has been sporadic and without pattern, it may point to an earlier-stage problem as opposed to a daily, habitual, ritualistic event that points to an entrenched addiction.

Medium

You should also ask specifically about the medium used to act out. Is it in print (yes, it does still happen) or on the phone, the laptop, the home computer, or school/work computers?

If it is on a smartphone, what apps are being used? You should press the issue here: examine what is on the phone and find out what has been deleted. Several apps used by kids today look innocuous on the surface but actually contain harmful material. For example, private photo vaults function this way. One such app appears to be a calculator, but entering the right passcode opens up a photo repository. Similarly, while many gaming and social media apps are not harmful in themselves, misuse can indicate a deeper issue and bigger problem.

As you can tell from this section, what we ultimately want is for both parent and child to understand what is really going on. While we want the behavior to stop, certainly, we also cannot overlook what is going on behind the scenes that drives the behavior. Look back to the section of the book on shame in Chapter 3 and view your child's acting out with that information in mind. This all helps inform what the next steps of help will look like.

Shelley's Thoughts

I believe one of the best things we can do for our children when it comes to these hard conversations is to make sure they understand how much we appreciate them being honest and vulnerable with us.

This starts early and with simple things. For instance, when my youngest comes up to me and shares that his brother pushed him, the best way I could respond would be as follows: I should take a deep breath, look into his eyes, and say, "Thank you for telling me." I've messed this up more than I've gotten it right; I normally say something like, "Seriously?! What happened? Why did he push you?" Yikes.

The last thing I want one of my children to believe is that it isn't safe to come to me with anything and everything in his heart and on his mind. This is the furthest thing from the truth—I want him to come to me without thinking twice! And yet, my usual not-so-great response clearly illustrates why one of my littles might think otherwise.

By expressing this gratitude and meaning it, not only do we set the tone for the conversation to be less about fixing and more about understanding, but we also pave the way for our kids to feel safe coming to us, no matter the situation.

Next Steps

Once you've gained some idea of the magnitude of the problem and the context wherein it exists, you can begin to decide on appropriate help. While every situation is unique, these three actions should be present throughout.

Creating a Safe Environment

While it seems as though it should go without saying, you need to be intentional here: creating an environment with your kids where you and they can ask questions without shame is critical. Make conversations about sexual integrity, awkward as they are, a regular part of touching base with your kids. Make it a point to follow up on the landmark conversation you have after discovery. Do not create a dynamic where it comes up, you talk about it, but then it's done, and you never talk about it again. This should be an ongoing, open-ended dialogue.

Teach your kids emotional language and model using it so they can give voice to the underlying heart issues that drive acting out. If you struggle to tap into your own emotions, there may be concurrent work to do here. The conversations you have while in the car or at the dinner table can give both you and your kids an opportunity to practice. Questions like these can facilitate growth in this area:

- What made you feel happy today?
- What made you feel sad or disappointed today?
- Did anyone do or say something that made you feel special today?

- Did you see any of your friends discouraged or encouraged today? If so, why?
- What are you most hopeful for or excited about today?
- If something was disappointing, how did you handle it? Did it make you cry?

You want to model asking and answering these questions and encourage your kids to answer for themselves. The more emotionally connected and self-aware they are, the less they'll feel the need to medicate.

Shelley's Thoughts

This modeling is a must. At our dinner table, we typically ask our boys the questions listed here: "What made you sad today?" "What disappointed you?" But the answers are classic: "Nothing." "I'm fine." "Pass the potatoes."

Jason or I almost always have to start the conversation. We share something from our days that made us feel sad or disappointed (or something else—fill in the blank with the emotion you're asking about). Without fail, the boys then start to chime in and talk about the things that made them feel sad or disappointed. It's shocking how going first and sharing our own emotions paves the way for our boys to genuinely and honestly share the feelings and perceptions they are dealing with deep within their hearts and souls.

Protective Boundaries

First on the list of protective boundaries is Internet filtering and monitoring. Every device should be covered by this. I talked about this in *Worthy of Her Trust* a bit—specifically, what these tools do:

> Internet filtering software allows you to customize the content allowed onto your device. It gives you the ability to block specific sites, categories, keywords, and domains. You can usually set access times and password protect certain programs.
>
> Internet monitoring software does not block anything; it simply records Internet activity. At specified intervals (for example, every two weeks) the software emails a report of Internet use to your accountability partners. I always recommend that the wife be one of the people getting that report.
>
> There are a couple of important things to know about these programs, though. First, there are always false positives. Something, at some point, will show up on the report that appears shady and maybe even out-of-bounds. However, it doesn't necessarily mean someone accessed that specific content directly. It could've shown up in a pop-up, a banner ad, or an in-page link.
>
> Some of the crazy naming mechanisms webmasters use can also trigger the program to flag a particular site. Anything in a report that looks suspicious should be discussed immediately.[10]

As it pertains to cell phones, filtering and monitoring software can also prevent apps from being downloaded, in-app purchases, access at certain times, and so on. Most of the filtering software out there also notifies the administrator (you!) if the software is deleted somehow.

This software does not apply to gaming devices or to the television, so I would encourage you to program the family/parental controls there as well to limit accessibility. Remember that on most gaming consoles, Internet access is only a couple of clicks away, which means pornography is only that far away. Likewise, the same goes for the TV. To that end, if you have any cable or satellite package that includes HBO, Cinemax, or adult channels—why? What in the world could be so important to watch that you'd put your children at risk for it?

The next layer of protective boundaries involves time and people. I can't tell you what is necessary at your house or what is age appropriate. Shelley and I decided that for our little kids, sleepovers are off-limits. That's just not something we're willing to accede to. It's a protective boundary. Yes, we've already been accused of being the weird parents with strict rules. So what? There are also certain friends we limit their time around. Shelley is selective about playdates with those kids because we know the parents have very different values than we do. Ultimately, you'll need to assess what boundaries are appropriate to protect your kids. It is very subjective, but I encourage you to err on the side of caution.

Realistically, we can't protect them from everything. But there are certain scenarios we can safely say should be avoided. Things like not having a computer in a child's bedroom or access to unfiltered Internet at home, and time limits and supervision with gaming are all boundaries to be considered.

Counseling

Depending on the situation, counseling for your child may be the next step. Young children in play therapy and older children in talk therapy sometimes say things they would never mention to a parent. Further, the nonjudgmental and partially anonymous environment can be conducive to helping the child willingly disclose deeper details. Per our previous discussion, the counseling should be consistent with the type of problem. If the sexual acting out is part of a systemic problem, the counseling should be angled at addressing the larger issue as well. It should be more holistic in approach. However, if your investigation concludes that the issue appears to be an acute sexual addiction problem, the counselor you choose should specialize in this area.

Prayer

It can be so easy to get caught up in the pain, confusion, and attempts to fix the problem that it hijacks your prayer life. For some people, the shame they feel as a parent can also preclude praying. I've talked to parents who recount how, when they had young kids, they didn't really think about praying for them. It wasn't until the kids became adults that it dawned on the parents to pray for them.

Whatever the case may be, we can take a cue from the life of Job. In Job 1:5, we find his commitment to his children's spiritual wellbeing: "Early in the morning he would sacrifice a burnt offering for each of them, thinking, 'Perhaps my children have sinned and cursed God in their hearts.' This was Job's regular custom."

Let us do the same, especially when we know our children are engaged in a struggle like this one.

Ultimately, you know your child best. You know when things seem off and out of character. If you find something suspicious or hear something that sounds suspect, don't hesitate to investigate. While your children are under your roof, one of your highest callings is to protect their souls. Few things are as harmful or have such a negative ripple effect as a warped sexuality.

Closing

If you find yourself in a relationship with someone struggling with sexual integrity issues, I'm sorry. I hate it for them, and I hate it for you. As we've discussed, there are few violations that feel as personally harmful and damaging as sexual betrayal. Whether it's a spouse or one of the kids, we want so badly to help, fix it, put it behind us, and move forward. Yet it leaves a permanent scar. It changes us and the person struggling.

I hope that through this book, you've gained nuggets of insight that help you see the person struggling with sexual integrity issues in a different light. He is not defined by his struggle, and you are not defined by your relationship with him. The person who is sexually addicted is hurting, living with a tumultuous inner world. He is deathly afraid of being fully known and rejected, yet he longs for acceptance to affirm his personhood. For many, the childhood scars on their hearts are still open wounds. Acting out sexually provides a Band-Aid and Advil, but the pain is still all too present and sensitive. Shame eventually becomes the driving force in their lives, informing everything from their faith journey to their engagement at work and home to their hobbies and interests, and it can even affect their physical health.

In the middle of all that, there are people like you, the reader, who wake up one day thrust into the vortex of this issue. You weren't asked for permission and didn't sign a liability waiver. Nonetheless, it demands your engagement. The willingness and humility of your loved one will, in many ways, determine the difficulty of your journey. You will be faced with some of the toughest decisions of your life regarding faith, forgiveness, and family. When all that dust settles, I believe God is still in the business of redemption. He is committed to showing us more about Himself and about ourselves. He is committed to developing us into greater likenesses and reflections of Himself. He wants to help us grow, to enlarge our capacity to love, and to increase our dependence on Him. My hope is that in the midst of the pain and the trials you are facing, you'll find Jesus more real, more powerful, and more gracious than you thought possible. And with that, you'll see yourself and the person you love who is struggling with sexual addiction more clearly through the eyes of Christ.

Suggested Resources

Video Curriculum for Couples—www.KitchenConvos.com
Support Groups for Wives—www.rlforwomen.com

Workshops for Men: Every Man's Battle Workshop—www
.everymansbattle.com
Workshops for Wives: Restore Conference—www.newlife.com

Counseling Services—www.redemptiveliving.com
Internet Filters—www.covenanteyes.com

Books

Worthy of Her Trust: What You Need to Do to Rebuild Sexual Integrity and Win Her Back—Stephen Arterburn, Jason Martinkus

Every Man's Battle: Winning the War on Sexual Temptation One Victory at a Time—Stephen Arterburn, Fred Stoeker, Mike Yorkey

Rescued: A Woman's Guide to Surviving and Thriving after Sexual Betrayal—Shelley Martinkus

The Summit Devotional—Jason Martinkus

Beyond Betrayal: How God Is Healing Women and Couples from Infidelity—Lisa Taylor

Shattered Vows: Hope and Healing for Women Who Have Been Sexually Betrayed—Debbie Laaser

Every Young Man's Battle: Strategies for Victory in the Real World of Sexual Temptation—Stephen Arterburn, Fred Stoeker, Mike Yorkey

(What to Do When He Says,) I Don't Love You Anymore—David Clarke, Ph.D.

Wired for Intimacy: How Pornography Hijacks the Male Brain—William M. Struthers

When Good Men Are Tempted—Bill Perkins

Your Sexually Addicted Spouse: How Partners Can Cope and Heal—Barbara Steffens, Marsha Means

Online Resources

www.redemptiveliving.com

www.newlife.com

www.fightthenewdrug.com

www.protectyoungeyes.com

Notes

1   "Porn in the Digital Age: New Research Reveals 10 Trends," Barna Group, April 6, 2016, www.barna.com/research/ porn-in-the-digital-age-new-research-reveals-10-trends/# .WMrHTDw0mWE.twitter.

2   "Porn in the Digital Age."

3   "APA's Vision, Mission, Values, and Goals," American Psychiatric Association, accessed October 12, 2017, www .psychiatry.org/about-apa/vision-mission-values-goals.

4   "AASECT Position on Sex Addiction," American Association of Sexuality Educators Counselors & Therapists (AASECT), accessed October 12, 2017, www.aasect.org/ position-sex-addiction.

5   William M. Struthers, *Wired for Intimacy: How Pornography Hijacks the Male Brain* (Downers Grove: Intervarsity Press, 2009), 105.

6   Steve Arterburn, Fred Stoeker, and Mike Yorkey, *Every Young Man's Battle: Strategies for Victory in the Real World of Sexual Temptation* (Colorado Springs: Waterbrook Press, 2015), 135.

7   Jason Martinkus and Stephen Arterburn, *Worthy of Her Trust: What You Need to Do to Rebuild Sexual Integrity and Win Her Back* (Colorado Springs: Waterbrook Press, 2014), 28.

8   Martinkus and Arterburn, *Worthy of Her Trust*, 27.

9   Shelley S. Martinkus, *Rescued: A Woman's Guide to Surviving and Thriving after Sexual Betrayal* (Castle Rock, CO: Open Sky Publishing, 2015), 39.

10   Martinkus and Arterburn, *Worthy of Her Trust*, 103.

For more information and resources, please visit

WWW.REDEMPTIVELIVING.COM

Kitchen CONV😀S

Take the guesswork out of the process and accelerate your healing.

THROUGH OVER 30 VIDEOS & THE INCLUDED WORKBOOK, THE COURSE PROVIDES PRACTICAL GUIDANCE & TOOLS TO WALK YOU THROUGH THE **HEALING PROCESS**.

- Disclosure/ discovery
- The grieving process
- How to handle anger and what role it plays
- Where relapse happens and how to avoid it
- The origins of Shame and how it drives acting out
- The Addictive Cycle and how to pull the ripcord and exit
- The Intimacy Aversion cycle and how we can engage rather than retreat
- How to handle triggers for wives / How to help your wife handle them
- How to rebuild deep, connected intimacy

KitchenConvos is an absolutely unparalleled resource for couples going through recovery and healing from sexual betrayal or addiction.

– LISA TAYLOR, CERTIFIED PASTORAL SEX ADDICTION SPECIALIST

WWW.**KITCHENCONVOS**.COM

NEWLIFE

Help in Life's Hardest Places

Talking about the things no one else will, to bring healing to those who've lost hope

"I have been living with my secrets for 30 plus years while failing time and again to stop and all the while them getting worse. For the first time I have learned more about why it is happening, developing an action plan to change, and creating a network of support."

— *Jack*
Intensive Workshop attendee

When you or someone you love is in crisis, you need a trusted friend to walk alongside you—a helper who's been there and understands, but who also has the training and skill to offer practical help.

New Life Ministries, founded by Steve Arterburn, exists to go into life's hardest places with you.

For over 30 years, we've provided expert answers to people just like you on our call-in radio show, *New Life Live!* We also offer a host of other resources, Intensive Workshops, and referrals to a carefully selected network of counselors.

Visit NewLife.com today to see how we can help, or call 800-HELP-4-ME. We want to hear from you!

NEW LIFE MINISTRIES EXISTS
TO GO INTO LIFE'S HARDEST PLACES

with you.

800-HELP-4-ME
NewLife.com

About New Life Ministries

New Life Ministries, founded by Stephen Arterburn, began in 1988 as New Life Treatment Centers. New Life's nationally broadcast radio program, *New Life Live!*, began in early 1995. The Women of Faith conferences, also founded by Stephen Arterburn, began in 1996. New Life's Counselor Network was formed in 2000, and TV.NewLife.com, the ministry's Internet-based television channel, was launched in 2014. New Life continues to develop and expand their programs and resources to help meet the changing needs of their callers and listeners.

Today, New Life Ministries is a nationally recognized, faith-based broadcasting and counseling nonprofit organization that provides ministry through radio, TV, their counseling network, workshops, and support groups, as well as through their numerous print, audio, and video resources. All New Life resources are based on God's truth and help those who are hurting find and build connections and experience life transformation.

The *New Life Live!* radio program, still the centerpiece of the ministry, is broadcast on Christian radio stations in more than 150 markets. It can also be seen on several network and online channels.

New Life's mission is to reach out compassionately to those seeking emotional and spiritual health and healing for God's glory. New Life Ministries Resource Center receives thousands of calls each month from those looking for help.

For more information, visit newlife.com.

About Stephen Arterburn

Stephen Arterburn, M.Ed., is the founder and chairman of New Life Ministries and host of the number-one nationally syndicated Christian counseling talk show *New Life Live!*, heard and watched by more than two million people each week on nearly two hundred stations nationwide. He is also the host of New Life TV, a web-based channel dedicated to transforming lives through God's truth, and he also serves as a teaching pastor in Indianapolis, Indiana.

Stephen is an internationally recognized public speaker and has been featured on national media venues such as *Oprah, Inside Edition, Good Morning America, CNN Live*, and *ABC World News Tonight*; in the *New York Times, USA Today, US News and World Report*; and even in *GQ* and *Rolling Stone* magazines. Stephen has spoken at major events for the National Center for Fathering, American Association of Christian Counselors, Promise Keepers Canada, the Lifewell Conference in Australia, and the Salvation Army, to name a few.

He is the bestselling author of books such as *Every Man's Battle* and *Healing Is a Choice*. With more than eight million books in print, Stephen has been writing about God's transformational truth since 1984. His ministry focuses on identifying and compassionately responding to the needs of those seeking healing and restoration through God's truth. Along with Dr. Dave Stoop, he edited and produced the number-one-bestselling *Life Recovery Bible*.

Stephen has degrees from Baylor University and the University of North Texas, as well as two honorary doctorates, and is currently completing his doctoral studies in Christian counseling. He resides with his family in Fishers, Indiana.

Stephen Arterburn can be contacted directly at SArterburn @newlife.com.

About Shelley and Jason Martinkus

Shelley S. Martinkus

Shelley has been married for sixteen years to Jason and has three little boys, Truman, Harrison, and Norman. Her entire world changed thirteen years ago, when she confronted Jason and demanded that he tell her the truth about his secret life of infidelity. Some of her darkest days after discovering the truth were also days that she'd never take back, because it was in this time that God revealed Himself to her in mighty ways. Little did she know, Jason's recovery would be the impetus for her to start to look honestly at her life, her past, and her brokenness and to seek healing and wholeness. Besides chasing after her three little boys, she is passionate about facilitating support groups for wives. Shelley regularly speaks at churches and workshops and is the national speaker for the Restore Conference. Her first book, *Rescued: A Woman's Guide to Surviving and Thriving after Sexual Betrayal*, was published in 2015.

Jason B. Martinkus, M.A.

After sexual addiction almost took his life and marriage, Jason was called to help other men. He received a bachelor's degree in finance from the University of Oklahoma and worked in the corporate world for companies such as Arthur Andersen and Interstate Batteries. After leaving corporate and going into ministry, he went back to school and received a master's in counseling from Denver Seminary. Today, he is the national speaker for Every Man's Battle and president of Redemptive Living, a Denver-based counseling and speaking ministry. He has dedicated his life to helping men find freedom from sexual integrity issues and couples find redemption beyond betrayal for their marriages. His first book, *Worthy of Her Trust: What You Need to Do to Rebuild Sexual Integrity and Win Her Back*, was released in 2014.

At David C Cook, we equip the local church around the corner and around the globe to make disciples. Come see how we are working together—go to **www.davidccook.com**. Thank you!

transforming lives together